ARMS CONTROL AND
THE ATLANTIC ALLIANCE:
Europe Faces Coming Policy Decisions

ARMS CONTROL AND
THE ATLANTIC ALLIANCE:

Europe Faces Coming Policy Decisions

KARL W. DEUTSCH

John Wiley & Sons, Inc.   New York · London · Sydney

To my children, *Margaret, Mary* and *Tom*
—my stakes and partners in the future.

Preface

IN 1963–1965, a group of political scientists at Yale University, in collaboration with scholars from several other institutions, undertook a study of current and prospective European attitudes to arms control and disarmament. Attention was concentrated on the present and expected future national attitudes and policies of France and the German Federal Republic, and on the prospects of these attitudes and policies being modified or replaced by any substantial steps toward European integration.

The evidence examined included extensive interviews with elite members in both countries, a survey of proposals for arms control and disarmament in Europe, mass opinion data, the content analysis of newspapers and periodicals, and data about the actual behavior of European states and populations in regard to international transactions.

The overall design of the research was based on two considerations. First, that France and West Germany are the decisive countries for the success or failure of arms control and disarmament, and of political integration, in Western Europe; that they are likely to remain so; and that what is acceptable to France and Germany is not likely to be rejected by the rest of Western Europe. Second, that the elites of France and Germany—even though each has considerable influence on the policies of its country—can exercise influence only within their respective national political and economic systems, and within the larger though looser system of Western Europe. The different types of evidence examined were designed to bring out the policy preferences and limitations of the French and German elites in this wider context.

This book deals primarily with the arms control aspects of the study. It summarizes briefly the design of the various relevant research operations and presents their chief results. The material on European unity, as well as on French and West German domestic politics, is presented at far greater length in another book, *France, Germany and the Western Alliance.*[1]

The research operations involved in this study were inevitably time-consuming, and so was the cross-checking of their results. Nevertheless, the main findings emerged rather quickly. Most of the preparation for the work began in the fall of 1963 and was completed by the spring of 1964. The elite interviews in France and Germany were conducted in the summer of 1964, and much of their punch card analysis followed in the fall. Most of the highlights of the findings became available for informal reporting in December, 1964, and January, 1965, for preliminary formal summarizing in April, 1965, and for a preliminary full-scale draft report in July, 1965. The period until January, 1966 was taken up with further cross-checking, verification, and editing of the findings in order to put them into a form best suited to the needs and interests of their readers.

This experience suggests that quantitative research methods, even on a fairly substantial scale, can be quick enough to yield interesting information about changing political conditions, but that the definite and detailed checking, extended analysis, editing, and presentation of findings tend to consume substantial additional amounts of labor, and, hence, time.

One example may suffice. Strong indications of the significant degree of French political support for President de Gaulle's opposition to the present arrangements in the North Atlantic Treaty Organization (NATO) were noted in December, 1964, and April, 1965, both in mass opinion and at the elite level. Any interested person could have known more than a year in advance of the likelihood of what the Paris correspondent of *The New York Times* reported on April 21, 1966.

> If United States policy-makers ever hoped that the French withdrawal from the integrated Western defense system could be slowed or reversed by appealing to the French electorate over the head of President de Gaulle, the last few days of sharp parliamentary debate should have disabused them. The debate showed that the President's hold on his followers, on Parliament and on the country has been strengthened rather than weakened by his attack on the North Atlantic Treaty Organization.[2]

[1] Karl W. Deutsch, Lewis J. Edinger, Roy C. Macridis, and Richard L. Merritt, *France, Germany and the Western Alliance*, New York, Charles Scribner's Sons, 1967.

[2] Henry Tanner, "A Stronger de Gaulle," *The New York Times*, April 22, 1966, 4:3–4.

The documents of the original study comprise several thousand pages of typescript, tables, and computer printout. In order to present a reasonably brief survey of its findings, a great deal of condensation has been necessary. This has applied not only to substance, with many tables and secondary matters omitted or mentioned only briefly, but also to language. In almost every paragraph, such qualifying phrases as "so far as this evidence goes," "it seems on the whole," "it appears by and large," or "making the best rough estimate in the light of the available data," should be taken as included. Using this cautious language of scholarship and diplomacy would have made this survey appreciably longer and a good deal more tedious to read. I have tried instead to use plain, declaratory statements wherever possible in reporting what seemed to me the conclusions of the evidence I had examined, and to present in most cases at least some of this evidence, together with each finding as indicated by the ensemble of the relevant data.

It can only be hoped that the reader himself, bearing in mind what has been said, will remember the phrases of caution and qualification tacitly present in each paragraph. Evidence deserves to be taken seriously; and the present study, despite its limitations of time and resources, has perhaps examined a larger body and a broader range of evidence than has been customary in academic studies in this field. The evidence, however, is by no means complete; and its interpretation is still a matter of fallible judgment.

With these qualifications in mind, it should be easier to accept the declaratory language of this brief survey. It is designed to focus attention on the main aims and questions pursued by this study, and on the main answers that have been found to them. Each of these answers, let it be repeated, is tentative; but in each case, the evidence seems to give the answer substantially more claim to attention and consideration than any alternative interpretations familiar from the literature of the subject.

My own interest in questions of international security and supranational integration has its roots in the study of nationalism which I began many years ago at Harvard University under the guidance of Rupert Emerson and Hans Kohn. This interest came to focus upon the problem of international security communities in the course of research which I carried out in 1953–1954 at Princeton University at the Center for Research on World Political Institutions, then headed by Richard Van Wagenen, whose initiative and leadership played a crucial role in the development of this then neglected field. Statistical methods for using data of trade and other international transactions were developed in 1956–1957 at the Center for Advanced Study in the Behavioral Sciences at Palo Alto, California, where I also became better acquainted with Harold Lasswell's seminal work on the study of elites. Finally, analytic concepts of integration, quantitative data, and methods for their analysis were developed at Yale University from 1958 with the help of the Carnegie Corporation and the National Science Foundation.

During the present study, on which most of this book is based, as well as in its preparation, I have become indebted for their collaboration and research contributions to Lewis J. Edinger, Roy C. Macridis, Richard L. Merritt, and Bruce M. Russett, as well as to Hayward R. Alker, Jr., Carolyn C. Cooper, J. Zvi Namenwirth, Ellen B. Pirro, Donald J. Puchala, Helga Voss-Eckermann, and others.

As Director of the study, Professor Richard L. Merritt made a crucial contribution to its cohesion and functioning. Important and helpful counsel and advice was received from Henry W. Ehrmann, Stanley Hoffmann, Daniel Lerner, Erwin K. Scheuch, and Adolf Sturmthal, as well as from Morton Gorden, Catherine McArdle, Rupert Breitling, Erwin Paul, Wolfgang Hirsch-Weber, and others. After the conclusion of the study, Daniel Lerner read a draft of the manuscript of this book.

The elite interviews were conducted in France by Roy C. Macridis, Bernard C. Brown, Henry C. Galant, and Robert Burton, and in the German Federal Republic by Lewis J. Edinger, Gerard Braunthal, Eugene C. McCreary, and Peter Merkl. Our colleagues in the Universities of Paris and Cologne, and at many other institutions of learning and centers of research, were outstandingly helpful in making this work possible.

Valuable assistance in editing and manuscript preparation was contributed by Mrs. June Darge, Mrs. Elizabeth Baskin, and Mrs. Lucille McKenna. For other assistance to the study I am indebted to the staffs of the Libraries and of the Computing Center at Yale University.

Research used in this book is drawn in part from materials prepared for the United States Arms Control and Disarmament Agency. It does not represent any judgment on the part of that agency or of any of its officials, or of any other agency of the United States government. The responsibility for all errors and weaknesses, for the summaries of research, and for all interpretations, inferences, and conclusions presented in this book remains unequivocally my own.

Karl W. Deutsch

New Haven, 1966

Contents

ARMS CONTROL AND
THE ATLANTIC ALLIANCE:

Europe Faces Coming Policy Decisions

1

Policy Choices on European Security and Arms Control

SINCE THE END OF THE SECOND WORLD WAR, the governments and peoples of Western Europe have had before them a choice of four major policies by which they might pursue the security of their political, social, and economic institutions against foreign military threats. (1) They could rely entirely upon the protection of the United States, at the price of gradually approaching the role of clients of that power, lobbying for decisions not of their own making. (2) Each of them could try to restore its national society and body politic, and eventually bear the burden of its own defense. (3) They could try to link an increasing part of their economies, their military establishments, and their political centers of decisions loosely by a system of alliances, in which each nation would retain its ultimate power of sovereign decision on matters of vital interest. (4) They could, by a substantial process of supranational integration, merge their institutions and identities ever more tightly into a single body, ruled in matters of major importance—such as war and peace—by a majority vote of a participating governments, if not peoples.

The first policy has been growing politically and psychologically irksome; the second policy has appeared prohibitively expensive and technologically unpromising. Consequently, much of the real debate about the best way to pursue European security has been between proponents of various forms of the third and fourth policies, that is, between men who thought in terms of alliance and those who thought in terms of integration.[1]

[1] For a highly suggestive discussion of many of the problems involved, see Henry A. Kissinger, *The Troubled Partnership*, New York, McGraw-Hill, 1965.

1

TABLE 1-1

An Overview of Alternative Approaches to European Security: National Sovereignty, Arms Control and European or Atlantic Integration (A Simplified Tabulation)

A. *French Elite Responses* (Figures in percent of total N, $N = 147$)

Attitude toward European or Atlantic Arms Competition versus Control	European Orientation				Atlantic Orientation			
	Arms				Arms			
	① Competition	② Control	③ DK	④ Subtotal Europeans	⑤ Competition	⑥ Control	⑦ DK	⑧ Subtotal Atlantics
I. Political sovereignty								
1. Independent national policy	3	3	0	5	6	1	4	12
2. Alliances among sovereign nations	1	5	1	6	1	3	1	5
3. Integration (political) part of the way	1	1	0	1	1	5	1	7
4. Integration (political) all the way to federation	2	8	0	10	2	8	0	10
5. Undecided on desired political status	2	6	1	9	1	2	2	5
Total I (Rows 1–5)	8	22	1	32	12	20	7	39
II. Military Integration								
6. For integration (military) conditional	2	7	1	10	2	4	3	10
7. For integration (military) unconditional	1	1	0	1	1	6	2	10
8. Not for military integration or undecided	5	15	1	21	8	10	2	20
Total II (Rows 6–8)	8	22	1	32	12	20	7	39
III. Overall integration SUBTOTAL I: Preservers of sovereignty (1 + 2)								
9. Complete	2	5	0	7	5	4	2	12
10. Ditto: Partial (for military integration)	1	3	1	5	2	1	3	5

| Pro-Europe and Pro-NATO | | | | Neither | Total I | Subtotals Arms | | | Total II |
| Arms | | | (12) Subtotal Pro-Europe and Pro-NATO | (13) Neither Europe nor NATO | (14) Community Views Columns 4 + 8 and 12 + 13 | (15) Competition Columns (1 + 5 + 9) | (16) Control Columns (2 + 6 + 10) | (17) DK Columns (3 + 7 + 11) | (18) Arms Views Columns (13 + 15 16 + 17) |
(9) Competition	(10) Control	(11) DK							
0	3	1	4	4	25	9	7	5	25
0	1	1	1	3	1	2	9	3	1
1	0	1	2	1	11	3	6	2	11
1	7	1	10	1	31	5	23	1	31
$\frac{1}{3}$	$\frac{0}{12}$	$\frac{1}{4}$	$\frac{1}{18}$	$\frac{2}{10}$	$\frac{18}{100}$	$\frac{4}{23}$	$\frac{8}{54}$	$\frac{4}{12}$	$\frac{18}{100}$
1	7	2	10	2	31	5	18	6	31
1	3	1	5	0	16	3	10	3	16
$\frac{1}{3}$	$\frac{2}{12}$	$\frac{1}{4}$	$\frac{3}{18}$	$\frac{8}{10}$	$\frac{53}{100}$	$\frac{14}{23}$	$\frac{27}{54}$	$\frac{4}{12}$	$\frac{53}{100}$
0	1	0	1	6	26	7	10	2	26
0	3	1	4	1	15	3	7	3	15

TABLE 1-1 (*Continued*)

A. *French Elite Responses* (Figures in percent of total N, $N = 147$)

Attitude toward European or Atlantic Arms Competition versus Control	European Orientation				Atlantic Orientation			
	Arms				Arms			
	① Competition	② Control	③ DK	④ Subtotal Europeans	⑤ Competition	⑥ Control	⑦ DK	⑧ Subtotal Atlantics
SUBTOTAL II: Integrationists								
11. Partial (at least 3 or 6)	3	11	0	14	3	12	3	18
12. Ditto: Complete (only 4 and 7)	0	0	0	0	1	3	0	3
SUBTOTAL III:								
13. Undecided on political and military status	2	4	1	7	1	1	0	1
Total III (Rows 9–13)	8	22	1	32	12	20	7	39
Dependence on U.S.								
14. Partial	1	1	0	2	4	2	3	10
15. Complete	7	19	1	28	6	12	4	22
16. No dependence seen or undecided	0	2	0	2	1	6	0	7
17. TOTAL IV (Rows 13–15)	8	22	1	32	12	20	7	39

Note: Rows Totals I–IV and Column Totals I and II are identical and are repeated for the sake of clarity. Minor discrepancies in subtotals and totals are due to rounding errors. More detailed tables with explanations are presented in Appendix A.

Alliances, like schemes for integration, could be seen as centered primarily on Europe, or envisaged as extending permanently across the larger North Atlantic Area. Moreover, security could be pursued in a context of a rising level of armaments, conventional as well as nuclear, in competition with the military and political efforts of the Communist bloc, or of particular Communist countries which might

| Pro-Europe and Pro-NATO | | | | Neither | ⑭ Total I | Subtotals Arms | | | ⑱ Total II |
| Arms | | | ⑫ Subtotal Pro-Europe and Pro-NATO | ⑬ Neither Europe nor NATO | Community Views Columns 4 + 8 and 12 + 13 | ⑮ Competition Columns (1 + 5 + 9) | ⑯ Control Columns (2 + 6 + 10) | ⑰ DK Columns (3 + 7 + 11) | Arms Views Columns (13 + 15 16 + 17) |
⑨ Competition	⑩ Control	⑪ DK							
3	5	2	10	2	43	9	28	5	43
0	3	1	3	0	7	1	6	1	7
0	0	0	0	1	10	3	5	1	10
3	12	4	18	10	100	23	54	12	100
0	1	1	1	2	15	5	4	4	15
3	11	3	17	4	71	16	42	8	71
0	0	0	0	4	14	1	8	0	14
3	12	4	18	10	100	23	54	12	100

also be in competition with each other. Or security might be sought within a stable or declining level of armaments, under some explicit or tacit pattern of arms control or actual disarmament.

A simple view of these analytical possibilities is presented in Tables 1-1 and 1-2, together with the percentages of German and French elite respondents whose answers in extended interviews during the

TABLE 1-2

An Overview of Alternative Approaches to European Security: National Sovereignty, Arms Control, and European or Atlantic Integration (A Simplified Tabulation)

B. *West German Elite Responses* (Figures 1s of total N, N = 173)

Attitude toward European or Atlantic Arms Competition versus Control	European Orientation				Atlantic Orientation			
	Arms				Arms			
	① Competition	② Control	③ DK	④ Subtotal Europeans	⑤ Competition	⑥ Control	⑦ DK	⑧ Subtotal Atlantics
I. Political sovereignty								
1. Independent national policy	2	2	0	3	0	1	0	1
2. Alliances among sovereign nations	1	2	0	2	2	6	0	8
3. Integration (political) part of the way	1	0	0	1	2	10	0	12
4. Integration (political) all the way to federation	1	7	0	8	6	13	1	20
5. Undecided on desired political status	0	3	0	3	0	2	0	2
Total I (Rows 1–5)	5	13	0	18	10	32	1	43
II. Military integration								
6. For integration (military) conditional	1	2	0	2	2	3	0	5
7. For integration (military) unconditional	3	11	0	14	8	24	1	33
8. Not for military integration or undecided	1	1	0	1	0	5	0	5
Total II (Rows 6–8)	5	13	0	18	10	32	1	43

| Pro-Europe and Pro-NATO | | | | Neither | ⑭ Total I | Subtotals Arms | | | ⑱ Total II |
| Arms | | | ⑫ Subtotal Pro-Europe and Pro-NATO | ⑬ Neither Europe nor NATO | Community Views Columns 4 + 8 and 12 + 13 identical with Columns 18 | ⑮ Competition Columns (1 + 5 + 9) | ⑯ Control Columns (2 + 6 + 10) | ⑰ DK Columns (3 + 7 + 11) | Arms views Columns (13 + 15+16 + 17) |
⑨ Competition	⑩ Control	⑪ DK							
1	1	0	1	1	6	3	4	0	6
0	5	0	5	1	17	3	13	0	17
1	5	0	6	3	22	4	15	0	22
2	11	1	14	3	45	9	31	2	45
1	1	0	2	3	10	1	6	0	10
5	23	1	28	11	100	20	69	2	100
1	2	0	2	2	12	4	7	0	12
3	14	0	17	2	66	14	49	1	66
1	8	1	9	8	22	2	14	1	22
5	23	1	28	11	100	20	69	2	100

TABLE 1-2 (*Continued*)

B. *West German Elite Responses* (Figures 1s of total N, N = 173)

Attitude toward European or Atlantic Arms Competition versus Control	European Orientation — Arms				Atlantic Orientation — Arms			
	① Competition	② Control	③ DK	④ Subtotal Europeans	⑤ Competition	⑥ Control	⑦ DK	⑧ Subtotal Atlantics
III. Overall Integration								
SUBTOTAL I:								
Preservers of sovereignty (1 + 2)								
9. Complete	0	1	0	1	0	0	0	0
10. Ditto: Partial (for military integration)	2	3	0	5	2	7	0	9
SUBTOTAL II:								
Integrationists								
11. Partial (at least *a* for 3 or 6)	2	5	0	6	3	17	0	20
12. Ditto: Complete (only 4 and 7)	1	5	0	6	5	9	1	14
SUBTOTAL III:								
13. Undecided on political and military status	0	0	0	0	0	0	0	0
Total III (Rows 9–13)	5	13	0	18	10	32	1	43
Dependence on U.S.								
14. Partial	0	0	0	0	1	1	0	1
15. Complete	5	12	0	17	9	30	1	40
16. No dependence seen or undecided	0	1	0	1	0	2	0	2
17. GRAND TOTALS: 1–5; 6–8; 9–13; 14–16 Subtotals I–III	5	13	0	18	10	32	1	43

Pro-Europe and Pro-NATO				Neither	⑭ Total I	Subtotals Arms			⑱
Arms			⑫ Subtotal Pro-Europe and Pro-NATO	⑬ Neither Europe nor NATO	Community Views Columns 4+8 and 12+13 identical with Columns 18	⑮ Competition Columns (1+5+9)	⑯ Control Columns (2+6+10)	⑰ DK Columns (3+7+11)	Total II Arms views Columns (13+15+16+17)
⑨ Competition	⑩ Control	⑪ DK							
0	1	0	1	2	4	0	2	0	4
1	5	0	5	0	19	5	15	0	19
2	10	1	12	6	45	7	29	1	45
2	7	0	9	1	29	8	21	1	29
0	1	0	1	2	3	0	1	0	3
5	23	1	28	11	100	20	69	2	100
0	0	0	0	0	1	1	1	0	1
5	21	1	26	8	90	19	63	2	90
0	2	0	2	3	9	0	5	0	9
5	23	1	28	11	100	20	69	2	100

summer of 1964 seemed to fall most nearly into the corresponding categories of policies endorsed. More detailed tabulations and comments may be found in Appendices A, B, and C.

Even this simple scheme suggests some things that are significant. It shows that a majority of French leaders—54%—supports arms control, and only 23% oppose it. Nearly one-half of the support for arms control, comprising 23% of all leaders, comes from leaders who also favor some form of supranational federation; but a majority of arms control supporters—or 30% of the total—hold fast to the essentials of a French nation-state, with only 6% willing to support some limited steps toward political integration.

These data suggest that as long as arms control is presented to the French leaders on its own merits, it commands majority support. When it is linked to supranational federation, however, it becomes a minority affair. Federalism is supported by only 31% of the French leaders. In its geographic aims it is divided in the classic manner into three parts: 10% wish primarily to federate Europe; another 10% prefer an Atlantic emphasis; and a third 10% desire to stress both. Regardless of geographic preferences, about four-fifths of the federalists favor arms control; only 5% prefer a competitive policy of armaments, evidently among supranational blocs rather than among nations.

A plurality of French leaders—41%—prefers a policy of national independence (25%) or of national alliances (16%). Another 11% are willing to combine this with partial steps toward supranational political integration, and another 18% are undecided, making a total of 69% (or 70%, were it not for rounding errors) of French leaders who are not prepared to accept political federation at this time.

Combining the problems of political and military integration sharpens the picture. A plurality of French leaders—43%—favors some limited steps toward integration, but only a handful—no more than 7%—are willing to go all the way to political and military integration in any kind of supranational community. The decisive margin for the acceptance of arms control in France must come from those French leaders who wish to hold onto much of the substance of French national sovereignty, but who are willing to accept within this framework some policies of international alliances, ultimate strategic dependence on United States nuclear protection, and substantial measures of international arms limitation or reduction.

The climate of opinion among the West German leaders is somewhat different in some ways, but similar in two essential points.

In the German Federal Republic, as in France, a majority of leaders supports arms control. Indeed, the German majority of 69% is substantially larger than the French one; the German opposition to arms control, at 20%, is smaller, and almost all German leaders express fairly clear-cut views on this subject. Furthermore, in Germany as in France, somewhat less than one-half of the support for control—31% of the total—comes from leaders willing to go all the way to federation. A majority of West German arms control supporters—38% of the total—are not ready to give up the essential sovereignty of the nation-state, although 15% are willing to accept some additional steps toward political integration. Here too, any close linking of arms control to European Atlantic federalism and to the substantial abolition of national sovereignty at this time means to deprive the cause of arms control of the majority support which it commands on its own merits.

Finally, in Germany, much as in France, some partial steps toward greater supranational integration, political or military, are endorsed by a strong plurality (45%). In contrast to France, two-thirds of West Germany's leaders favor unconditional military integration, and nearly one-third (29%) profess all-out integrationism, both political and military.

The complete strategic dependence of their country on the United States is perceived by large majorities in both France (71%) and Germany (90%). In both countries, these majorities also include most of the opponents of arms control. Since preference for arms competition thus goes together with a sense of complete strategic dependence on the United States, the minorities who do not favor arms control would find it hard to oppose once it becomes clear-cut United States policy. Conversely, more than one-half of the small minorities who deny or minimize the ultimate strategic dependence of their country on the United States still favor arms control. Thus an American policy emphasizing a plausible combination of arms control and continuing ultimate American protection for Western Europe could command very wide support among the elites of both France and West Germany.

Though perhaps thought-provoking, this scheme is clearly much too crude. To get an even moderately better understanding of the problems of arms control in the European political environment, we shall need to know a great deal more about the more specific policy alternatives as perceived by the elites of France and Germany; and we shall need to know a great deal more about the background conditions in economic and social transactions, press communications, arms control proposals, mass opinion data, and the like—all of which bear upon the policy choices among national independence, international alliance, or supranational integration, and between higher or lower levels of armament. It is these matters which were explored by analyzing various types of quantitative evidence, then further explored in extended interviews with over 300 French and German leaders in the summer of 1964, with results set forth in the body of this study.

THE CENTRAL QUESTIONS

The study aimed at answering two groups of questions.

1. To what extent should Western Europe be considered a system of nation-states, and to what extent an emerging integrated political community, a new supranational political unit, or an eventual federation? What, in particular, are the relations of France and West Germany to European integration and to one another?

2. In this problematic European political environment, what steps or proposals for the limitation and control of armaments, for the relaxation of international tensions, and for eventual disarmament, are most likely to be accepted or rejected? Why? By whom?

In one sense, almost everyone has an answer to the first question. It is obvious, according to some writers, that there is a basic trend toward European integration which has long passed the point of no return. It seems equally apparent to other observers that the trend toward European integration has halted in recent years. Presumably it is also obvious to at least some others that European integration has remained limited chiefly to peripheral and surface matters and has left essentially untouched the cores and basic structures of political, military, and financial sovereignty of the major West European nation-states, as well as of their national systems of mass communication and political opinion.

What is lacking are not guesses that seem obvious to those to whom they appeal, or to those whose particular experiences they may fit. Rather, what is needed is broadly based evidence that may serve to confirm, or at least substantially strengthen the case for one or more guesses, while invalidating, or at least substantially weakening, the case for seemingly no less plausible alternative interpretations.

In principle, the task of this study was similar to the second question. Since in public debates on both sides of the Atlantic disarmament and arms control in Europe have been less salient than European integration, no clear-cut competing guesses have become established as alternative interpretations in the public mind. If the debate on these topics should continue, however, such competing estimates would be likely to appear. One writer might say that it was obvious that Europeans feared all talk about arms control and the relaxation of international tensions, since it implied the threat of an American-Soviet bargain at the expense of European interests, or at the expense of the national interests of particular states, such as the German Federal Republic. Other writers would then be likely to assert that, on the contrary, it was certain that Europeans desired above all the relaxation of tensions and the reduction of the burdens and risks of armament. Still other interpretations might seem no less manifest to their propounders. Here again, a broad survey of evidence would be desirable, not necessarily to discover a wholly new perspective, but at the very least to discover which of the several seemingly plausible perspectives was in better accordance with a broader range of facts, and perhaps which ones appeared to remain genuinely open.

Evidence and Methods

To seek answers to these questions, several bodies of evidence were examined. These included data about actual transactions among West European nations, such as trade, mail, travel, migration, and the exchange of students, and their levels and changes, chiefly during the period 1928–1963. They also included data from a survey of arms control and/or disarmament proposals made by governments, responsible officials, or important public figures in France, Germany, Britain, the United States, or the Soviet Union during the years 1945–1964.

Third and fourth bodies of evidence were obtained from the content analysis of editorials on European integration in four leading newspapers, from France, Germany, Britain, and the United States, for the years 1953 and 1963; and from another and broader survey of editorials on arms control from over 100 newspapers and periodicals published shortly after ten key events relevant to arms control and disarmament during the period 1946–1963. Still another body of evidence was obtained from the analysis of a considerable number of public opinion surveys in France, Germany, Italy, Britain, and to a small extent from the United States, chiefly for the period 1952–1964.

Finally, 147 carefully selected members of the French political elite and 173 similarly selected members of the elite of the German Federal Republic were interviewed in the summer of 1964 for an average of one and one-half hours each. The interviews were carried out as far as possible in an informal atmosphere but in accordance with a carefully worked out schedule of questions in order to insure relevance and comparability. The results were recorded, coded on punched cards, and subjected to intensive analysis. The results of this analysis were made available to the leaders of the French and German interview projects to be checked against their own impressions and evaluations.

CONCLUSIONS DRAWN FROM THE FINDINGS

All the lines of evidence pursued in the inquiry tend to converge. Although there are minor differences, the weight of evidence points in the same direction on at least six major points.

The movement toward structural European unification since 1957 has been largely halted or very much slowed down. The next decade of European politics is likely to be dominated by the politics of nation-states, and not by any supranational European institutions. In this regard and for this period, the view of President de Gaulle, that only nation-states will be obeyed and supported by the population, and the view of M. Raymond Aron, that there will be no European federation—even for the next twenty years—seem to be born out by the great preponderance of all the data examined.

Within France and Germany, the attitudes of various elite groups generally were closer to each other, and to the mass opinion of their own country, than to the opinion of their counterparts in the other country. Nationality continued to be a far stronger determinant— or indicator—of political attitude than did class, age, occupation, religion, party affiliation, and even, for most respondents, ideology. At present, it appears that the nation-states are continuing their hold on the minds of both leaders and masses in Western Europe, and they are likely to continue to do so for the next decade.

A provisional factor analysis of the elite survey data confirms this finding. Its results suggest that nationality seems to be between two and ten times as powerful as any one cross-national factor, such as religion, occupation, socialist party affiliation, etc., in accounting for the distribution of responses. To restore once again in the mid-1960s the vigor and momentum of the years 1947–1955 to the movement toward European unification would require much larger efforts on the part of European nations and of the United States than seem to be contemplated now in any quarter of authority. It might require economic input of a scale as large as that of Marshall Plan aid in relation to the shrunken European economies of 1948, and hence it might have to be correspondingly larger in 1965. It would require a priority of American attention fixed on Europe rather than on Asia and a shift of emphasis from the predominantly military to broadly inclusive economic, cultural, and social patterns of integration; and it would also require a reorientation of the priorities of attention and policy of the French and West German elites and governments. No indication of the likelihood of any of these changes is currently in sight.

There is not enough general consensus between France and West Germany to sustain a major common policy, and even less a common body politic, either at the level of mass opinion or at the level of the elites. The development of such a consensus is likely to require far more than ten years, even under favorable conditions.

Alliances, particularly with the United States, and limited steps toward additional supranational arrangements and institutions are popular among elites and acceptable to mass opinion. National isolationism is being rejected, but increasing national equality—or perhaps a share in great power privilege—is being demanded, particularly by the elites of France.

There is striking consensus in France and Germany on the desirability of arms control and disarmament, including further direct agreements between the United States and the Soviet Union. There is particularly strong consensus on the desirability of halting the spread of nuclear weapons to nations which do not now possess them.

There is at present strong opposition in Germany to the acquisition of national nuclear weapons, and there is no strong positive desire for any German share in a nuclear weapons system through some multilateral arrangement, such as the MLF project. And there is overwhelming and deep-rooted French hostility to any idea of a German national nuclear weapon, or to a substantial German share in a multilateral nuclear weapons system.

Under these conditions of European politics, the most nearly acceptable approach to arms control and disarmament might be an international agreement limiting the possession of nuclear weapons to those five powers now possessing them: the United States, Britain, France, the Soviet Union, and Communist China. With the exception of Communist China, these are the governments in control of those countries whose special importance is recognized in the United Nations Charter by giving them the status of Permanent Members of the United Nations Security Council. The legal status of Communist China is currently blocked in this respect, but her acquisition of a nuclear device has been tacitly tolerated by all other nuclear powers, and an explicit or tacit nuclear *modus vivendi* with Communist China does not seem unacceptable to European leaders.

Even without an agreement with China, an antiproliferation agreement and extended nuclear test ban among the "Big Four"—the United States, the United Kingdom, France, and the Soviet Union—might prove feasible, and might pave the way to further steps toward arms control. Such an approach might meet some of the French desire for a full and genuine share in international leadership. The study data suggest that such an accommodation of French desires on the part of the United States and Britain would be acceptable to the majority of the West German leaders.

2

The Halting of European Integration
Since the Mid-1950s

SINCE THE MID-1950s, European integration has slowed, and it has stopped or reached a plateau since 1957–1958. An analysis of trade data, going back as far as 1890, suggests that in the 1957–1958 period European trade reached the highest level of structural integration. Most of this level was reached by 1954, but there were slow advances until 1957–1958. Europe is now much more highly integrated than it was between the Wars or before the First World War, but since 1957–1958 there have been no further gains. The absolute increases after 1958 in trade, travel, postal correspondence, and the exchange of students are accounted for by the effects of prosperity and by the general increase in the level of these activities themselves. There have been no increases in integration in regard to all these transactions beyond those one would expect from mere random probability and the increase in prosperity in the countries concerned.

The spectacular development of formal European treaties and institutions since the mid-1950s has not been matched by any corresponding deeper integration of actual behavior. As far as they go, the data do not suggest that any substantial increase in European integration should be expected by 1970 or 1975, even among the Six, if the practices and methods of the 1950s and the early 1960s are merely continued. The expectable pattern for the next ten years, as suggested by a study of the trends in European transactions from 1928 to 1963, is toward a Europe of national states. These will be linked by marked but moderate preferences for mutual transactions, with little growth—and possibly some decline—in the intensity of those preferences as

17

expressed in actual behavior of the populations and business communities of the European countries.

The foregoing observations apply with particular strength to France. France alone of the European Economic Community countries has retreated in part from foreign trade. It now has a lower proportion of foreign trade to national income—28% in 1963—than it had in 1928, when the proportion stood at 38%, whereas her trade with the other EEC countries remained unchanged at about 10% of her national income in both years. France has thus retained a greater amount of national self-preoccupation than have Germany, Italy, and Benelux countries.

A different line of analysis of economic data suggests, on the basis of provisional computations, that Western Europe has traversed about half of the way toward structural economic integration and that perhaps another 40 years might be needed, at rates of progress from 1913–1955, to complete the process.* In any case, the pace of actual progress seems much slower than the pace of such legal and theoretical timetables as those in the formal treaties of integration. Difficulties in implementing these timetables after 1965 may be in part inherent in this underlying situation.

The Decline of Interest in General Designs for European Unification

THE EVIDENCE OF THE ELITE PRESS. The impression of a halt in the growth of integrative sentiment in Europe is confirmed by a content analysis of "prestige" newspapers. For the years 1953 and 1963, *Le Monde*, the *Frankfurter Allgemeine Zeitung*, *The Times of London*, and *The New York Times*, were selected as the most representative elite newspapers of France, West Germany, Great Britain, and the United States, respectively. All editorials in these papers dealing with European or Atlantic integration or European politics in general were identified; a sample of 200 editorials was chosen by appropriate procedures and was subjected to intensive content analysis by computer. The main changes found in the relevant editorials of each elite paper from 1953 to 1963 were the following.

Interest in Atlantic Alliance, a primarily military association set against the background of a bipolar world, has declined markedly in all three European papers. This decline is moderate but clear in the *London Times*. It is greater in the *Frankfurter Allgemeine*

* This 40-year period is suggested by unpublished provisional results of research by Robert Schaefer, Yale University, 1965–1966.

Zeitung (FAZ) and greatest in *Le Monde*. All three European papers have moved toward greater concern for European integration, seen in economic terms against the background of an increasingly multipolar world. Only *The New York Times* has not shared in this trend. Its editorials alone intensified their Atlantic and military emphasis and their view of the world as a continuing bipolar power system.

There has been a decline in the attention of all four papers to any general political or legal designs for a unified Europe, and a corresponding shift to greater concern with concrete difficulties of European integration or cooperation in regard to such matters as agriculture. In 1963, only *The New York Times* continued to maintain a reduced, although still marked preponderance of interest in idealized political or legal designs for a unified Europe.

The concern with domestic French and German controversies, as opposed to any attention given to the requirements and costs of supranational alliances, remained unchanged in all four papers over the ten-year period. According to some theories of political integration, if there had been major progress toward supranational integration during that decade concern with domestic controversies should have been expected to decline, and the interest in the needs of supranational alliances to increase. No evidence of such a shift was found.

In all four papers, concern increased from 1953 to 1963 in regard to United States pressure for the extension of the powers of supranational organizations, particularly within an Atlantic framework. By 1963, supranational integration had become more closely identified with United States initiatives and pressures. On this issue, *The New York Times* alone shifted from an attitude of moderate but marked concern for American initiatives and pressures for European unification in 1953 to a much stronger emphasis in 1963. In the latter year, it seemed to be living in a different world from that of the European papers.

The chief form of United States activism, as discussed in these editorials, referred to American efforts to merge military and economic supranational instrumentalities in Europe or in the Atlantic area. Such a linkage between economic and military policies appeared in 1963, however, as a theme chiefly created by American speakers and writers, with no substantial support in any of the European papers studied. References to arms control and disarmament in all four papers were so rare in the editorials on European politics and integration that no statistical analysis could be undertaken in regard to these topics. These problems were not seen, it appears, in the context of European unity and general European politics.

THE EVIDENCE OF MASS OPINION.   A considerable number of French and German public opinion polls for the years 1952–1962 were analyzed for the purpose of making comparisons between the two countries, as well as comparing political attitudes among different groups and making comparisons with a smaller number of similar polls in Italy and Britain.   Methods used included the charting of time trends with the help of graphs and factor analysis with the aid of computers.   From these analyses several tentative findings emerged.

There was persistently greater elite and mass attention to national concerns, rather than to European ones.   Large samples of Germans were asked year after year by German interviewers, "What is the most important task before our country?"   In the spring of 1965, 47% said "national reunification," and 4% said "Berlin," whereas only 3% said "European union."   National interests outpolled European interests fifteen to one—and had done much the same for more than a decade.

Throughout the period 1954–1962, the difference between French and German mass opinion tended to be larger than between opinion in either country and that of Italy or Britain, or between British and Italian attitudes.

Friendly feelings in French mass opinion about Germany and in German mass opinion about France increased substantially to roughly one-half of the Germans and Frenchmen polled in 1963–1964.   Feelings of mutual trust increased much less, to about one-fifth of the respondents in each country.   Answers in the mid-1950s to the specific question, "Which country would you trust as an ally in case of war?" showed markedly greater trust of France and Germany in Britain, and even greater trust in the United States, than among those two continental countries.

Questions about the Western alliance in peacetime, and about the same alliance in case of war, revealed marked decreased in support by French or German mass opinion for the latter and more serious eventuality, but a slight increase in the British popular commitment. Nevertheless, factor analysis of many French and German opinion poll results between 1954 and 1962 indicated a marked increase in the similarity of underlying images between the two countries, as expressed by the amount of variation which could be accounted for by factors common to both countries.   In particular, between 1954 and 1962 there was a marked increase in the importance of an image of a United Europe in both French and German opinion.   Most of this increase occurred between 1957 and 1962.   During the same years, there occurred a marked decline in the perception of any military threat and of the danger of nuclear war. Increased interest in European unity thus appeared quite compatible with a decreased sense of military danger.

The greater similarity of French and German perceptions in 1962 than in 1957 and 1954 was not matched, however, by any net increase in the similarity of French and German political values. Although Frenchmen and Germans had come to agree to an increased extent on what they saw in the world around them, they continued to disagree on what they liked.

The strongest difference between French and German mass opinion in the analysis of these particular surveys was found in the area of international politics. Germans had a clearly favorable image of the Western alliance and a clearly unfavorable one of the Soviet Union, whereas the French attitude toward symbols of Western unity or a "Western camp" was negative in 1962, and their anti-Russian posture was conditional and reserved. French popular opinion became increasingly pessimistic from 1957 to 1961, and in the confrontations of 1962 it continued to blame the United States for world insecurity, while being divided in blaming the Russians for recklessness. German mass opinion, however, in the same situation saw United States policy as directed toward world security, and saw the Russians as acting recklessly. Generally, German mass opinion was markedly pro-American, while the French majority was so only with reservations, and a sizable minority gave outright anti-American responses.

Only in regard to accepting European unity, at least in general terms, Frenchmen and Germans agreed to a greater extent in 1962 than they had done in earlier years. Even here, however, on the specific questions of European political unity and federation, French mass opinion remained significantly less "European" than its German counterpart.

The over-all impression from the analysis of the trend of French and German mass opinion data from 1954 to 1962 is that of opinion halting or hesitating at a threshold. There is a consensus that European unity is a good thing, and that some steps should be taken to maintain and strengthen what European unity there is and to go further in that direction. Mass opinion seems to bear no clear image of what these steps should be, or how far they should go, and there is no sense of urgency about them.

Thus there is now in European mass opinion a latent clash between the continuing acceptance of the reality of the nation-state, and the newly accepted image of some vague sort of European unity. The ensemble of these present public moods may facilitate general expression of good will, combined with policies of temporizing, caution, national consolidation, and only gradual and sectoral advance toward somewhat greater European integration.

THE EVIDENCE OF ELITE INTERVIEWS, 1964. Since the results of the elite interviews conducted in the summer of 1964 with 147 French and 173 West German respondents as well as the interpretations and judgments of their authors are discussed at considerable length in the full report and Appendix A, only a few major points will be summarized here.*

FRENCH: PERSISTENT NATIONALISM WITH MAJOR CLEAVAGES. French elite responses show the continuing strength of self-assertive nationalism. Nearly seven-eights of the respondents see current French policies as increasingly nationalistic, and nearly three-quarters see the world as an increasingly multipolar power system, replacing the earlier bipolar United States-Soviet predominance. Three-fifths definitely approve this trend, and a majority asserts a "manifest density" for France.

There is overwhelming French elite consensus on *not* trusting Germany beyond a very limited extent. This consensus was expressed in many ways throughout most of the interviews. Only 7% of 136 articulate French leaders are willing to trust the German Federal Republic "a great deal." Of the 109 French leaders who express their views on German reunification, only 7% favor it unconditionally, and of the 77 French leaders who comment on its security aspects, 58% consider it a threat to French security.

On many issues, outright nationalist views command only strong minority support. A plurality of nearly one-half flatly deny that Europe will be unified within the next ten years, and 41% choose national predominance as their preferred form of European integration, as opposed to 43% who want supranational influences to predominate. Only 30% endorse an independent national foreign policy for France, whereas 70% prefer a policy of alliances.

* Percentages given in this summary are based on all respondents, including those who said "don't know," as well as those who did not comment on the particular question, *if* this category amounted to no more than 5% of the total. If a larger proportion did not touch on a particular question, the percentages given refer only to the "articulate" respondents, that is, to those who did make a comment, even if they only professed themselves to be undecided or uninformed. In this latter case, the actual number of articulate respondents on the question is indicated.

Efforts toward some further limitations on national sovereignty are favored, at least conditionally, by 83% of French leaders, and definitely so by 45%, with only 14% even conditionally in opposition. French elite consensus seems more favorable to at least some limited further steps toward supranational collaboration than have been the recent policies of President de Gaulle. During the next few years, such limited steps might be expected to be undertaken by himself or his successors with elite support.

The basic pattern of national self-assertion and of French elite preferences and expectations seems likely to persist, however. Current (i.e., relatively strained) French policies toward the United States and NATO were most often mentioned (29%) as likely to continue after President de Gaulle.

French domestic cleavages also seem certain to persist. Less then one-fifth of the respondents turned out to be clear-cut Gaullists. Although a majority expected that the Fourth Republic would not be restored, and that some institutions of the Fifth Republic would survive de Gaulle, there was no agreement on just which features would survive. The hopes for a more pragmatic and consensual "new politics" in France have not materialized.

An analysis of elite groups by age indicates that no major changes are likely to occur over the next ten years. Typically, age accounts for less than 5% of the variance in the answers found. Within these limits, the "middle elites"—those in their fifties and hence the generation of the 1930s and the Second World War—tend to differ from both their elders and their juniors, who in turn often resemble each other. This middle elite group is somewhat more nationalistic and more closely identified with the de Gaulle regime.

The junior elite—those under 50—are more internationalistic, more in favor of alliances, and still more opposed to an independent foreign policy for France. A moderate shift toward a more internationalistic foreign policy might be supported by this generation once its members win full power in the 1970s, but the essential features of French politics are likely to remain.

French elite members themselves do not expect to change their minds. An above average degree of closure of thinking is reported for 70% of the respondents, and only 1% feels that the policies proposed by them for defending the French national interest might become impractical in the future.

A brief follow-up survey was taken among the same group of respondents in December, 1964, after Khrushchev's fall, President Johnson's election, and the Chinese nuclear explosion. It elicited about 60% usable responses and confirmed the stability of French attitudes expressed in mid-1964.

WEST GERMANS: STRENGTHENED NATIONAL CONSENSUS AND GREATER READINESS FOR SUPRANATIONAL STEPS.   Elite consensus on definite satisfaction with the present West German regime and its basic policies includes nearly three-quarters of West German respondents.   Adding those indicating moderate satisfaction brings total elite support for the German Federal Republic regime at 93%.   This support extends solidly across all groupings of age, class, occupation, major party, and past political record.

In contrast to their more detached or alienated French counterparts, large majorities of West German elite members see themselves as influential in the policies of their own country, and appear more likely to identify with these policies.   As recorded by interviewers, 73% of German respondents indicate that they think they have more than average influence in domestic affairs, and 66% do so in regard to foreign policy, in contrast to only 33% and 18%, respectively, among the French.

The foreign policy of the German Federal Republic is definitely supported by 55% of the West German leaders, in contrast to France whose current foreign policy is clearly supported by only 33% of French elite respondents.   West German support for "all features" of current foreign policy, and particularly for the alliance with the United States, was expected to continue beyond Chancellor Erhard's term of office.

West German leaders are in overwhelming agreement on their country's need for allies: 93% see alliances and international instrumentalities as the best means for defending the national interest of their country.   Only 7% name national instrumentalities, and only 6% favor an independent national policy.   Enduring common interests with the United States are stressed by 72%, and 71% favor policies aiming at further reductions in national sovereignty.

In contrast to France, two-thirds of the West German leaders continue to see the world as a bipolar system, dominated by the United States and the Soviet Union, and they believe that it will remain so.   Among the French leaders, however, nearly three-quarters see an increasingly multipolar world around them.   Faith in a continuing bipolar world is somewhat weaker among West German politicians (58%), and it is shared only by a minority of German civil servants (44%).

There is less agreement among German leaders about just how far these internationalists policies will go, or ought to go. A strong plurality—46%—expect European integration to be achieved within the next ten years, while 35% consider this unlikely. A predominantly supranational form of European union, if it should come to pass, is chosen by a bare majority of the respondents, but 45% prefer "confederation" or arrangements implying the clear-cut predominance of nation-states. In France, only 19% expect European union within 10 years, whereas 49% explicitly do not; and 56% of the respondents prefer confederation or national predominance.

Not unconnected perhaps with the increased strength of the West German army, German elite support for the 1954 project of a European Defense Community (EDC) of conventional forces has changed by 1964 to definite opposition by a plurality, 44% against only 35% in clear support. In France, a much smaller trend seems to have gone in the opposite direction; 23% of the French leaders now definitely favor EDC, and only 18% clearly oppose it.

CONTRASTING FRENCH AND WEST GERMAN VIEWS OF FUTURE CHANGES. French response patterns generally indicate that the Fifth Republic is not perceived as deeply rooted, and that many pre-Gaullist institutions and forces, such as the old political parties, are expected to reassert themselves after President de Gaulle's departure from political activity. French leaders thus expect short-run changes after de Gaulle, restoring a considerable measure of long-run continuity in society and politics.

German leaders, on the contrary, expect the trends of change, initiated by the Bonn Republic, to continue beyond Chancellor Erhard's tenure of office, and in large majority they expect no return or revival of any of the pre-Bonn political forces or practices from the Nazi or Weimar periods. As many as 86% of articulate respondents consider Nazism dead; 73% see the possibility of an SPD (Social Democratic Party) government within the next ten years, and 40% consider it likely; but in any case a majority feel sure that it would make very little difference to domestic or foreign policies, except at most in regard to personnel recruitment.

French and German elite expectations differ strongly in regard to German reunification, as well as to European union. Of the 173 German leaders, only nine do not comment on this point, while over one-third of the French do not. Among articulate German respondents, 20% definitely expect reunification to take place within the next 25 years, but only 2% among the articulate French do so. Another 38% of the Germans have at least conditional hopes for reunification within the next quarter century, but only 11% of the French agree with them; and 83% of the Frenchmen commenting consider German reunification as at least unlikely within that period.

Concerning European unification, a plurality of 46% of the 158 articulate German elite members see it as likely to succeed or at least make substantial progress within the next ten years, but only 19% of the 141 articulate French leaders share this view. By contrast, no success of, nor any substantial progress toward, European union within the next ten years is expected by 35% of the articulate German leaders but by as many as 49% of the French.

ATLANTIC ALLIANCE AND EUROPEAN ASPIRATIONS. French and German leaders agree—90% in Germany and 72% in France—that the ultimate military security of their countries depends "completely" or "in large measure" upon the deterrent force of the United States. Most German respondents use the stronger, and most Frenchmen the more cautious, wording. Large majorities of articulate respondents—79% in Germany and 65% in France—feel sure that the United States is unlikely to abandon its commitments to the defense of Western Europe. Even larger majorities in both countries refer to long-run common interests, linking their nations with the United States.

There is also agreement among 65% of the German and 62% of the French elite respondents that NATO can be relied upon completely or to a considerable extent. The stronger alternative is more popular in Germany, and the weaker one in France. Minorities of 18% of the German and 30% of the French leaders, however, prefer to rely on NATO only "to a limited extent" or not at all.

Large majorities—68% in Germany and 63% in France—agree that Britain ought to be included in an integrated Europe. A majority of 52% in France stress long-term common interests with Britain, but only 28% do so in Germany.

The same elite proportion of 28% in Germany stress common long-term interests with France, and 37% in that country feel they share common long-run interests with Germany. In addition, common interests with the other five EEC members, including Germany and France, respectively, are emphasized by 88% of the French and 35% of the German elite members.

The result is somewhat paradoxical but in line with other evidence. Majorities of French and German leaders see their countries linked more strongly by long-run political and military interests to the United States—and in the second place to Britain—than to one another. Any weakening of French ties to the United States thus might weaken the German-French relationship. In distinction from the views of

President de Gaulle, the majority of French elite respondents prefer to keep these links to the United States strong, if this could be done on terms nearer to political equality.

French aspirations to a greater measure of equality divide many French and German views on NATO. Among articulate French leaders, 78% favor NATO reforms in this direction, and only 2% say no reforms are needed. Among their German counterparts, only 47% desire such reforms, and 38% consider all NATO reforms unnecessary.

When asked to choose between policies of strengthening mainly European institutions, such as EEC, and strengthening NATO, 40% of the 124 articulate French respondents prefer EEC, whereas only 4% favor NATO. The 141 articulate Germans are split more evenly, with 15% picking EEC and 11% choosing NATO, but a 72% majority refuses to choose and insists on supporting both—a middle way favored also by a French plurality of 49%. Major attempts by President de Gaulle or any successor to pit in a forced choice "Europeanism" against "Atlanticism" are thus likely to run into strong elite opposition in both countries.

Despite this reluctance of French and even more of German leaders to choose between Atlantic and European alignments, it seems from many subtle indications that the latter had come to command by 1964 much the larger share of elite imagination and emotional involvement. The vision of a rich, multidimensioned, and growing Atlantic Community has faded.

DIFFERENTIATED VIEWS OF COLD WAR PROBLEMS AND INTERNATIONAL RELAXATION. French and German elite members strongly agree in seeing Communist states and activities as the greatest threat to the security of their countries, and in opposing the withdrawals of troops or nuclear weapons from Central Europe. The neutralization of Central Europe is definitely opposed by 69% of the 166 German elite members who expressed their views, but only by a plurality of 38% of the 71 Frenchmen who did so.

Despite the perception of a Communist threat, European integration is seen as primarily nonmilitary in purpose. Strengthening the West against Communism is seen as the purpose of European integration only in 19% of the French and 10% of the German responses, while 45% of the French and 67% of the German replies emphasize economic and cultural purposes.

There is near-record consensus among both French and German leaders that in the next few years relations between their nations and "the countries of Eastern Europe" will become more cordial. No fewer than 99% among the 118 articulate French respondents say so, and so do 83% of the 162 articulate German leaders, including large majorities in all occupational elite groups in both countries.

There is much less support, however, for the familiar proposals to relax international tensions by formally recognizing either the division or the current boundaries of Germany. Of the former measure, only 25% of 153 articulate Germans and 18% of 55 articulate French leaders think that it might ease international tensions. Recognition of the Oder-Neisse boundary with Poland is seen as probably helpful in easing such tensions by a majority of 52% of the 155 articulate Germans, but only by a plurality of 42% of the 52 French leaders who commented on this matter.

On the whole, French and German leaders produce parallel majorities on six out of ten questions relating to the Cold War complex, but in most cases they differ even there in regard to salient points and perhaps in underlying expectations. A majority of German respondents favors a partial continuation of the "hard line" policies of Cold War days, in the hope that these will ultimately lead to success, or to desirable changes, in the bipolar struggle; the French leaders seem to back the same policies, with much greater detachment, in the expectation that they might best preserve the German *status quo* in a multipolar world.

It is against this background of manifest and latent differences in French and German views (some of which will be discussed in Chapter 4) that current and prospective French and German responses to arms control and disarmament proposals have to be appraised.

3

Proposals for Arms Control in Europe and Their Press Reception

A SURVEY OF SIXTY-FOUR PROPOSALS, made between 1947 and 1964, for arms control or disarmament in Europe, included both official propoasls and major public suggestions of political leaders, parties, or respected writers.[1] Its findings are subject to the limitations that only those proposals that were specifically focused on Europe were considered, that repetitions or minor variations of old proposals were excluded, and that some proposals may have been overlooked. Nevertheless, it seems likely that all salient Europe-centered proposals were included. The survey shows the following.

French interest in arms control has been much lower than that of any other major country. During the 18 years covered, there were only four French proposals, two of which were made in 1959 by out-of-office political leaders Pierre Mendes-France and Jules Moch. No official French proposals were found after 1956, and no significant French proposals from any source after 1959. In order of frequency, proposals came most often from the Soviet Union (18) and the United States (14), followed by Britain (11), the German Federal Republic (10), Poland (7), and, at a considerable distance, France (4).

[1] See Bruce M. Russet and Carolyn C. Cooper, "A Review of Major Proposals for Arms Control in Europe" (New Haven, Yale University, mimeographed, 1966).

THE SHIFT FROM EUROPEAN TO WORLDWIDE
STEPS TOWARD DISARMAMENT AND ARMS CONTROL

Over three-fifths of the proposals made by government spokesmen
of some kind, and nearly nine-tenths of the proposals from opposition
leaders or private persons, fell into the five-year period from 1955
to 1959. During this peak period, official Western and East Bloc
propoals were equally frequent. From 1960 onward, Europe-oriented
official proposals from the United States diminished; Britain and Western Germany made no such official proposals at all, and, by criteria
of relevance for this report, they contributed only one unofficial proposal apiece; and France contributed nothing at all. United States
policy turned toward worldwide approaches to arms control, such
as the nuclear test ban of 1963. The East Bloc countries (i.e., the
U.S.S.R., and Poland), however, continued in 1961–1964 to make
Europe-centered proposals at nearly the same rate as 1955–59, with
a somewhat larger share coming from Poland. Details are given in
Table 3-1.

This undiminished East Bloc activity might have the possible effect
of preempting some of the role of champion of disarmament from
the East Bloc countries, at least in relation to Europe. It might also
associate to some extent the entire topic of arms control with East
Bloc propaganda in the minds of West European elite members, thus
reinforcing the partial withdrawal of their interest from this topic. If
United States proposals for Europe should become salient and frequent,
Western European elite interests might again increase. To some extent, the shift of United States policy to worldwide proposals for
arms control and disarmament has taken interest away from local or
regional plans for Europe. This shift is well in accord with the preferences of majorities of French and German leaders. It nevertheless
leaves open the possibility that European arms control problems, such
as those posed by the MLF proposal, may interfere with East-West
agreement on worldwide measures, such as a nuclear antiproliferation
treaty, and that the Soviets may still appear as the particular champions
of arms control in Europe.

Independent evidence for the possible existence of such a situation comes from mass opinion data. In the early summer of 1964 a
sample of more than 1800 West Germans was asked who most of
all was talking about disarmament; the replies are recorded in
Table 3-2.

TABLE 3-1*

Major Proposals for Arms Control and Disarmament in Europe, 1947–1964, by Periods and Countries

(Additional proposals from opposition leaders or private persons are given in parentheses.)

Year	U.S.	U.K.	West Germany	France	Total West	U.S.S.R.	Poland	Total East	Total — Opposition Official or Private
1947	1				1	1		1	2
48									
49	1				1				1
50									
51									
52									
53									
54			(1)		(1)	1		1	1 (1)
55	(3)	2	(1)		3(1)	2		2	5 (1)
56	2(1)	1	(2)	1	2(5)	2		2	4 (5)
57	1	(1)	1(1)	1	3(3)	2	1	3	6 (3)
58		1(3)	1		3(3)	1	2	3	6 (3)
59	1(2)	1(1)	(2)	(2)	2(7)	3		3	5 (7)
60									
61	1		(1)		1(1)	4	1	5	6 (1)
62							1	1	1
63						2	1	3	3
1964	1	(1)			1(1)		1	1	2 (1)
Total	8(6)	5(6)	2(8)	2(2)	17(22)	18	7	25	42 (22)
Summary									
I 1947–54	2	0	(1)	0	2(1)	2	0	2	4 (1)
II 1955–59	4(6)	5(5)	2(6)	2(2)	13(19)	10	3	13	26 (19)
III 1960–64	2	0(1)	0(1)	0	2(2)	6	4	10	12 (2)
Total	8(6)	5(6)	2(8)	2(2)	17(22)	18	7	25	42 (22)

* Based on data from Bruce M. Russett and Carolyn C. Cooper, "A Review of Major Proposals for Arms Control in Europe" (New Haven, Yale University, mimeographed, 1966), Appendix.

TABLE 3-2

Who Talks about Disarmament? German Mass Perceptions, 1964
Question: "One often hears talk about disarmament. Who is talking about it most of all?"

| | Party Preference (in percent) | | | | |
	SPD	CDU/CSU	Other (i.e., mainly FDP)	None	Total
The Russians	41	39	31	29	38
The Americans	27	26	41	20	26
The SPD	8	4	3	2	5
The German Federal Government	4	4	6	4	4
The CDU/SDU	1	1	1	1	1
The Berlin Senate	1	1	1	1	1
Don't know; no reply	18	25	17	43	25
Total	100	100	100	100	100
Number of respondents	626	799	102	306	1,833

Source: Institut für Angewandte Sozialwissenschaft (ifas), Bad Godesberg, Germany, Letter by Klaus Liepelt, August 4, 1964.

THE SUBSTANCE OF THE PROPOSALS FOR EUROPE

In regard to the substance of arms control and disarmament proposals for Europe, three distinct periods or stages—1945–1954, 1955–1958, and 1959–1964—again seem to stand out.

These substantive trends are substantially summarized by Bruce M. Russett and Carolyn C. Cooper.[2]

"National policies toward problems of arms control in Central Europe have gone through three fairly distinct periods. The first extends from the end of the Second World War through perhaps 1954. During this time there seemed to be a significant consensus between East and West as to certain prerequisites for a formal agreement: Germany must be reunified, but neutralized so that she would not again threaten the peace of Europe. To

[2] *Op. cit.*, with minor editorial changes.

complete the latter assurance the earlier plans put forth both by the United States and by the Soviet Union called for the German state to be unarmed though later versions would have permitted her some non-nuclear weapons under international control. No agreement of course was reached during this period, largely because of quite differing interpretations of what reunification or neutralization were to mean in practice—how, for instance, the former was to be accomplished, what the role of the German Communist Party would be, and what kinds of guarantees would be required.

"The second period can be dated from the ratification of the Paris Agreements in May 1955, or possibly somewhat earlier. From the creation of the West German army, and NATO's dependence upon it for any hope of a successful conventional defense of Europe against Soviet attack, virtually all official Western proposals abandoned the earlier commitment to neutralization, and called instead for a reunified German state free to choose its orientation. With three-fourths of the population of the prospective state coming from the Federal Republic, such a choice was almost certain to be for the NATO alliance. And however much it might have been hoped that eventually a negotiating position of strength might be established so as to impose such a solution, it was clear that at the time this proposal was quite unacceptable to the Russians. Only with some sweeping concession in another area of the world could such a proposal possibly be made palatable, and no such sweetener was ever proffered. At most some Western plans offered to keep East German demilitarized in the event that the country as a whole chose NATO. This policy, nevertheless, had the firm support of the West German CDU government, was frequently reiterated by the United States, and only rarely departed from by the British or French governments.

"But the British Labour Party and the German SPD, with the relative freedom from constraint enjoyed by opposition parties, held instead to the original Western position—for a Germany both reunited and neutral, with its arms level subject to some form of international control. The goals of these two groups, however, were compatible rather than identical. The SPD sought a means, acceptable to the Russians, of achieving reunification; Labour's primary goal was the political and military stabilization of Central Europe, reducing the spectre of inadvertent war arising from a revolt in East Germany or a clash between the two German

states.   Yet the Russians were not very amenable to this sugges-
tion either.   Although they occasionally intimated a willingness
to consider it (and thus kept up some German hopes that they
might someday negotiate a deal), they had much to gain from
keeping East Germany's economic and military potential within
their own alliance.   Most Eastern proposals during this time
called in effect for ratification of the political *status quo*, but
within various controls over armament levels and especially the
prohibition of nuclear weapons on German soil.   Many official
proposals, on both sides, were useful primarily for the public
record and perhaps for the contest for German loyalties.

"The third phase can perhaps be traced to Hugh Gaitskell in
1958 when, without abandoning Labour's commitment to a united
neutral Germany as a worthwhile "long-term objective," he proposed interim arrangements for inspection and the reduction of
troop levels within the area of a Germany still divided and its
separate states allied to East and West.   By 1961 this concern
had clearly supplanted, in official Labour policy, the earlier concern for German reunification.   The shift undoubtedly stemmed
from the growing threat of nuclear weapons in Germany, the
danger that these weapons might wind up in German hands, and
Labour's special sensitivity to nuclear arms.   This concern was
nevertheless manifested elsewhere in the Western camp: in the
French Left (the proposals of Moch and Mendes-France in 1959),
eventually in the SPD, and even in the British Conservative Party
(note "interim" proposals by leading Tories in 1959 and 1964).
Only the United States and West German governments have
held firm to the original negotiating position—the CDU undoubtedly because it fears to give up any bargaining counters
(such as a relaxation of military tensions in the center of Europe)
without achieving its primary goal, reunification, and the United
States from its need for West German troops in NATO and its
desire not to antagonize its Bonn ally.   Certainly there are also
serious military considerations, such as the potential loss of the
tripwire or the physical difficulties of basing NATO troops elsewhere than in Germany, which contribute heavily to this position.

"Throughout the last decade the official Western position has
demanded two elements—Germany's reunification, and no restric-
tions on its alliance.   The Russians have as vividly indicated that
while they might consider either (and have in fact offered both,
singly) the combination is unacceptable.   Negotiations have never
reached the point where either side seems actually to have made

provisions for committing resources to carry out what it proposed. Interestingly the question of inspection, on which so many other arms control proposals have foundered, has not been an immediate stumbling block, at least not on the surface. The Soviet Union, in fact, has discussed inspection procedures in greater detail than have most Western plans, though of course great difficulties might arise if the negotiations ever got down to this level.

"In the past four years there have been no further American proposals specifically addressed to arms control in Europe. Although the Russians, Poles, British, and, to a lesser degree, the Germans, have continued to address the question, American interest has shifted sharply to such functionally (rather than geographically) defined problems as the test ban and worldwide arms reduction."

THE PRESENT MOOD

There seems little likelihood of any East-West agreement for the reunification of Germany in the foreseeable future. Some of the major protagonists would agree to the principle of German unity only on terms unlikely to be accepted by the other side. The Labour Party and the SPD have now adopted a position on German alliance which coincides with that of the West German and American governments. The Soviets have made unmistakable their rejection of this position. Plans for the withdrawal of foreign troops and creation of a neutral belt in Central Europe, championed by the SPD, Labour, and the Poles in the late 1950s, appeared quite dead by 1964.

But opportunities for agreement on limited arms control without a political settlement seem somewhat more fluid. At the same time that they abandoned their hope for a neutral reunified Germany, Labour and the SPD sharpened their interest in an interim agreement on the control of nuclear weapons in Europe. Although the realities of trying to hammer out an agreement might quickly dispel any illusions, it would seem that in principle the Soviets share this concern. Until now CDU fears of compromising eventual German reunification have prevented exploration of such interim measures in any important degree. Yet the American government has long had an interest in surprise attack precautions and other measures which could possibly be treated separately from the question of Germany's future, and such a separation may well be a consequence of this interest.

It is against this background of rising press attention to arms control and disarmament in general, and of declining diplomatic interest in arms control plans specifically centered on Europe, that the relevant attitudes of French and German elite members have to be evaluated.

To survey leading editorial reaction in France, West Germany, Britain, and the United States to the issues of disarmament and arms control, a large number of newspapers and periodicals in these countries were analyzed. This particular content analysis operation was carried out by "hand" methods, focusing upon editorial responses to specific proposals or events relevant to disarmament or arms control. For this purpose, a list was compiled of the ten major arms control or disarmament proposals or events that had received the largest amount of press attention. The first five items spanned the years from the Baruch Plan of 1946 to the Rapacki Plan of 1957, and the second five items, the years from Khrushchev's speech in 1959 to the nuclear test ban in 1963. A list of these events is given in Table 3-3. For editorial comments on these ten events, 97 newspapers and periodicals were searched, 35 from the United States, 29 British, 16 French, and 17 West German. A total of 655 issues were consulted for the relevant periods, and 370 editorials were found and analyzed.[3]

Of these ten most salient events between 1946 and 1963, as defined by the amounts of editorial attention they attracted, nine dealt with worldwide aspects of disarmament or arms control, and only one—the Rapacki Plan of 1957—was specifically limited to Europe. During roughly the same period, 1947–1964, at least 64 distinct Europe-centered arms control or disarmament proposals were counted in a survey carried out for this study, but 63 of them did not become as prominent in the newspapers as the ten arms control events selected. European and American press attention, it appears, continued to see disarmament and arms control primarily as worldwide rather than European problems.

Press reactions to these ten events were categorized in three different ways. The simplest categorization is along the *time* dimension: the ten events were divided into two groups of five each. Thus, the earlier time period, from 1946 to 1957, includes the Baruch Plan, the Anglo-French Memorandum, the Soviet 1955 Proposals, the "Open Skies" Proposal, and the Rapacki Plan. The later time period, from 1959 to 1963, includes the Khrushchev Speech, French Testing, Soviet Testing, the Kennedy Speech, and the Test Ban Treaty.

A second categorization is based on the *source* of the proposal or event. There are, first of all, proposals stemming from Western

[3] Lists of events and publications, as well as detailed methods and results are presented in Richard L. Merritt and Ellen B. Pirro, "Press Attitudes to Arms Control in Four Countries, 1946–1963" (New Haven, Yale University, mimeographed, 1966). All data and tables in this chapter are taken from this work.

TABLE 3-3*
Brief Descriptions of Ten Most Salient Arms Control and Disarmament Events, 1946–1963

1. The *Baruch Plan* (June 4, 1946): the first major disarmament proposal after World War II to receive serious attention; it called for the creation of an International Atomic Development Authority within the framework of the United Nations to exercise widespread control over the production and use of atomic energy.

2. The *Anglo-French Memorandum* (June 11, 1954): this proposal, submitted to the Sub-Committee of the U.N. Disarmament Commission as a possible basis for compromise, asked for a ban on the use and production of nuclear weapons and other weapons of mass destruction, the conversion of existing stockpiles to peaceful uses, major reductions in armed forces and armaments, and an international control commission.

3. The *Soviet Proposals of May 10, 1955:* this plan aimed at the prohibition of use and production of nuclear weapons, provided for staged reduction of armed forces and conventional arms, called for the establishment of a control organ, and proposed an inspection system.

4. President Eisenhower's *"Open Skies" Proposal* (July 21, 1955): this proposal for mutual aerial inspection and the exchange of military blueprints by the U.S. and the U.S.S.R. gave top priority to finding a mutually acceptable system of inspection and reporting.

5. The *Rapacki Plan* (October 2, 1957): this plan, in its initial form, proposed the prohibition of the production and stockpiling of nuclear weapons in Poland and both parts of Germany. (This was the only one of the ten most salient arms control proposals which was specifically limited to Europe.)

6. The 1959 *Khrushchev Speech* at the U.N. (September 18, 1959): this lengthy address advocated general and complete disarmament, an urgent search for an agreement to end nuclear testing, and a system of international control; it also mentioned several previous Soviet proposals, including those of May 10, 1955.

7. The initiation of *French Testing* of atomic weapons (February 13, 1960): the first French atomic explosion took place in the Sahara.

8. The resumption of *Soviet Testing* (August 30, 1961): the Soviet Union resumed nuclear testing and terminated the "moratorium" of 1958–1961.

9. The *Kennedy Speech* on the resumption of U.S. testing (March 2, 1962): this radio-television address announced that the United States would resume atmospheric nuclear tests if agreement could not be reached early in the meeting of the new Eighteen Nation Disarmament Committee in Geneva.

10. The Limited *Test Ban Treaty* (Signed August 5, 1963): this U.S.-U.K.-U.S.S.R. treaty called for the cessation of nuclear weapon tests in the atmosphere, in outer space, and underwater and was subsequently signed by over 100 countries (France and Communist China being significant exceptions).

Source: Richard L. Merritt and Ellen B. Pirro, "Press Attitudes to Arms Control in Four Countries, 1946–1963" (New Haven, Yale University, mimeographed, 1966).

* Any good library is likely to contain the full texts of these ten documents.

sources (i.e., the United States, the United Kingdom, and France); and, second, some proposals from Eastern European sources (i.e., the Soviet Union and Poland). For this categorization the Test Ban Treaty of 1961 was listed as a Western and an Eastern Event. This is simply because, as far as the press of the world was concerned, the treaty was not primarily the product of any single country. An alternative solution might have been to refrain from categorizing it at all, but this would not have altered the findings significantly. Finally, the two events that represented actions rather than proposals or agreements were grouped independently of the other two classifications: these were the French initiation and Soviet resumption of nuclear testing.

The Increasing Attention to Disarmament and Arms Control

Within the selected periods following major disarmament-related proposals or events, the general issue of disarmament and arms control was perceived as fairly important. Over the entire peroid 1946–1963, editorial responses were found in an average of 58% of the journal issues examined for the four countries.

Among these countries, most attention to arms control problems was paid by the press of the German Federal Republic (77%) and of France (61%), followed by that of Britain (48%) and the United States (45%). To the extent that these differences reflect reader interest, rather than accidents of the study's crude sample selection, they may indicate the existence of a significant reservoir of public interest in disarmament and arms control in Germany and France.

Over several years, interest in arms control and disarmament rose substantially in all four countries, from an average of 43% for the

TABLE 3-4
General Attitudes toward Arms Control and Disarmament, 1946–1963

	France	West Germany	United Kingdom	European Average	United States	Four Country Average
Favorable	76%	53%	74%	68%	48%	63%
Unfavorable	5	0	1	2	1	2
Neutral/other	19	47	24	30	51	35
Total	100	100%	99%	100%	100%	100%
N	(63)	106)	(86)	(255)	(115)	

four countries during 1946–1957 to 70% for the years 1959–1963. Interest thus rose by an average of 63% from the earlier level. The increase was strongest for Germany and Britain, weaker for the United States, and weakest—but still of considerable size—for France, where the frequency of editorial attention to arms control and disarmament events rose from one-half of the relevant journal issues in the first period to two-thirds in the second. Detailed figures are given in Table 3-4.

Emotional Concern and Support for Arms Control and Disarmament

Emotional involvement was substantial and increased over time. Such involvement was communicated in three-fourths of the editorials on arms control events in the first period, and in about two-thirds of those in the years 1959–1963. Emotional involvement was highest for the United States, high for France and Britain, and low but rising for West Germany. The general attitude toward efforts at disarmament or arms control was overwhelmingly friendly, with 60% of all mentions favorable and only 1% opposed. The distribution of favorable and unfavorable editorial responses is given in Table 3–4.

The data show a striking similarity in German and United States responses in contrast to the press attitudes in France and Britain. The percentage share of expressed general sentiment in favor of arms control and disarmament declined slightly over time in all four countries, and there were corresponding moderate increases in the relative expressions of skepticism and cynicism. Changes over time appear in Table 3-5.

These limited increases in skepticism and cynicism were clearly outweighed, however, by the substantial increase in general attention to arms control and disarmament. The latter effect in 1959–1963 occurred largely at the expense of the share of neutral or noncommittal editorials in the earlier period, and it was so strong that the net share of expressed pro-ACD sentiments actually became larger. The increase in attention to ACD events was further reinforced by an increase in emotional involvement in all countries except France.

Increases in regard to attention, emotional involvement, and over-all pro-ACD views were smallest for France and largest for West Germany. During 1946–1957, France led in net pro-ACD sentiment, followed by the United States and Britain, with West Germany in last place. In 1959–1963, on the contrary, West Germany was first in the net proportion of pro-ACD editorials, followed again by the United

TABLE 3-5
Attitudes toward Arms Control and Disarmament Events: Changes over Time

	France		West Germany		United Kingdom		United States		Average	
	Pro-ACD	Anti-ACD	Pro-ACD	Anti-ACD	Pro-ACD	Anti-ACD	Pro-ACD	Anti-ACD	Pro-ACD	Anti-ACD
a. Over-all view										
1946–57	72%	17%	43%	20%	65%	15%	74%	17%	63%	17%
1959–63	49	29	54	16	56	15	63	23	56	21
Net pro-ACD shift	(−23)	(−12)	(+11)	(+ 4)	(− 9)	(0)	(−11)	(− 6)	(− 7)	(− 4)
b. Emotional involvement										
1946–57	61	6	17	7	53	12	64	17	49	11
1959–63	36	27	30	16	50	15	66	24	46	21
Net pro-ACD shift	(−25)	(−21)	(+13)	(− 9)	(− 3)	(− 3)	(+ 2)	(− 7)	(− 3)	(−10)
c. Perceived operationality										
1946–57	50	0	7	3	38	0	25	0	30	1
1959–63	15	11	0	2	34	10	21	0	18	6
Net pro-ACD shift	(−35)	(−11)	(− 7)	(+ 1)	(− 4)	(−10)	(− 4)	(0)	(−12)	(− 5)
d. Likelihood of acceptance										
1946–57	33	22	17	27	12	56	11	49	18	39
1959–63	33	47	0	21	9	41	4	38	12	37
Net pro-ACD shift	(0)	(−25)	(−17)	(+ 6)	(− 3)	(+15)	(− 7)	(+11)	(− 6)	(+ 2)
e. Perceived sincerity										
1946–57	56	6	27	0	65	0	74	4	56	3
1959–63	40	27	21	3	41	18	42	17	36	16
Net pro-ACD shift	(−16)	(−21)	(− 6)	(− 3)	(−24)	(−18)	(−32)	(−13)	(−20)	(−13)
f. Long-run effects										
1946–57	83	0	33	3	68	0	55	2	60	1
1959–63	40	20	33	12	50	8	40	8	41	12
Net pro-ACD shift	(−43)	(−20)	(0)	(− 9)	(−18)	(− 8)	(−15)	(− 6)	(−19)	(−11)

Note: The above figures include testing events where appropriate. Plus signs show pro-ACD shifts; minus signs show anti-ACD ones.

TABLE 3-6

Changes in Attention, Emotional Involvement, and Net Pro-ACD Sentiment in the Press of Four Countries, 1946–1963*

	A. Attention per cent of press issues examined		B. Emotional Involvement (Per cent of editorial mentions)		C. Over-all Pro-ACD Sentiment (Per cent of editorial mentions)		D. Net Pro-ACD Responses (Per cent of all issues, i.e., $A \times C$)	
		Rank		Rank	Pro-ACD	Rank	Pro-ACD	Rank
1. *France*								
Period I, 1946–57	50	2	67	2	72	2	36	1
Period II, 1959–63	67	2	62	3	49	4	33	4
Change, period I to II	+17	4	−5	4	−23	4	−3	4
2. *West Germany*								
Period, 1946–57	51	1	23	4	43	4	22	4
Period II, 1959–63	96	1	46	4	54	3	52	1
Change, period I to II	+45	1	+23	1	+11	1	+30	1
3. *United Kingdom*								
Period I, 1946–57	35	4	65	3	65	3	23	3
Period II, 1959–63	63	3	65	2	56	2	35	2.5
Change, period I to II	+28	2	0	3	−9	2	+12	2
4. *United States*								
Period I, 1946–57	37	3	81	1	74	1	27	2
Period II, 1959–63	55	4	90	1	63	1	35	2.5
Change, period I to II	+18	3	+9	2	−11	3	+8	3
5. *Total-all papers*								
Period I, 1946–57	40	–	64	–	64	–	26	–
Period II, 1959–63	69	–	69	–	56	–	39	–
Change, period I to II	+29	–	+5	–	−8	–	+13	–
6. *Average, four countries*								
Period I, 1946–57	43	–	59	–	64	–	27	–
Period II, 1959–63	70	–	66	–	56	–	36	–
Change, period I to II	+27	–	+7	–	−8	–	+9	–

* Calculated from figures in Merritt and Pirro, *op.cit.* Since publications of each country are being read primarily within that country, it seems misleading to take the total of all papers and then to weight any one country more if more papers or periodicals from it are examined, as is done above. It seems better to weigh all countries equally, and use the simple average of four countries. As rows 5 and 6 of the table show, however, the difference between the results of the two methods of computation is slight.

41

States and Britain, with France now least friendly to arms control. Before 1957, France was first in net pro-ACD press sentiment, and West Germany was last. After 1959, this was reversed, with West Germany now first, and France in last place. The United States and Britain continued to rank in the middle. Even in France, however, as in all four countries, pro-ACD views clearly prevailed over anti-ACD ones in the second period also.

An increase in gross pro-ACD sentiment occurred only in West Germany, together with a much larger increase in ACD attention than in any of the other three countries. The combined effect of these two changes put West Germany first in net pro-ACD sentiment during 1959–1963 (see Table 3-6).

EAST-WEST PARTISANSHIP AND DIFFERENCES AMONG ALLIES

The emotional attitudes toward specific propoasls were fairly evenly divided. They were positive in just one-half of the evaluations of the Eastern proposals and in about two-thirds of the Western plans. The pro-Western bias was strongest in the press of the United States and France, weaker in Britain, and, surprisingly enough, weakest in West Germany, where the press was almost equally cautious in treating all proposals, regardless of source. In the course of time, there were few substantial changes in partisanship. The greatest decline occurred in French trust in Western arms control proposals, and in British trust in Russian and Polish ones.

Specific arms control proposals were treated most often as serious and sincere, despite a minority current of comments labeling many of them unrealistic or propagandist. (Perceptions of sincerity or insincerity of proposals are relevant for only seven of the ten arms control and disarmament events, since the Test Ban Treaty of 1963 and the French and Soviet nuclear tests of 1960 and 1961, respectively, appeared not as proposals but as accomplished facts.)

In 1959–1963, in contrast to the 1946–1957 period, the belief in the sincerity of arms control proposals decreased slightly for the Kennedy speech, which was the only Western proposal, but somewhat more for the Khrushchev speech, which was the only proposal from the East tabulated for the second period. Together with the larger relative share of Eastern proposals in the second period, this produced a marked decline in over-all perceptions of the sincerity of arms control proposals for the more recent period. Even here, however, the over-all perceptions of sincerity outweighed those of insincerity by more than two to one for Eastern proposals, and, less surprisingly, by more than three to one for proposals coming from the West.

As targets of attention, Russia, the United States, and France were the countries whose names and comments received the most attention over the period as a whole, accounting for about two-thirds of all national comments reported. They were followed by Britain, Red China (and other Asian Communist countries), and West Germany, and further, at a considerable distance, by scattered references to other European nations, other West European nations, the East Asian allies of the United States, and the members of three other Asian and African regional groupings. Emotional attitudes in the editorials of each country toward other nations varied. Toward the United States they were about 30% friendly and 60% neutral. Toward the Soviet Union they were most often negative (56%) or else neutral (34%). Toward Britain they were almost equally friendly (41%) or they were neutral (44%). Toward France and Germany they were predominantly neutral.

Countries perceived as allies tended to get somewhat less attention than those seen as adversaries, such as Russia or Communist China. The attention-getting power of the United States, however, constituted a partial exception. There was a frequent tendency in the press of the United States, France, and Britain, respectively, to pay most attention to the proposals of its own government, and less attention to the proposals or moves of other countries. Although there were some exceptions—the German press paid a great deal of worried attention to many moves by other countries—the evidence confirms the familiar picture of the national press of each country often conducting a kind of national monologue rather than genuine cross-national communication within the Western alliance.

The attitudes and attention patterns of the French and German press were not distinctly more similar between these two countries than they were between any one of them and either Britain or the United States. For the average of 38 aspects of attitudes to arms control events, both in 1946–1957 and in 1959–1963, there were only moderate differences in the similarity between the members of each of the six possible pairs among the four countries. Among the six possible pairs of countries, however, the French-German pair ranked sixth in terms of similarity in 1946–1957, and fourth during 1959–1963, while the United States-Britain pair consistently ranked first. In regard to these matters, as far as this particular evidence goes, the differences between the French and German press have remained substantial.

4

Changing Images of Danger: Cold War versus Relaxation

FRENCH AND GERMAN ELITES STRONGLY agree in seeing Communist states and activities as the greatest threat to the security of their countries, and in opposing the elimination of nuclear weapons from Central Europe, or the withdrawal of troops from that area. On these three topics, the majorities of articulate elite respondents are 76, 63, and 61% for France, and 70, 65, and 72% for Germany, respectively. In both countries, the perception of a Communist threat is strongest among the 50 to 60 year-old leaders, but whereas the difference is large in France (91%, against 70 and 69 for the Senior and Junior elites, respectively), it is only slight in West Germany (57%, against 53 and 54%, respectively, for the Senior and Junior elites).[Q.62, by age]

French fears of the Communist countries were strongest among politicians (87%) and the military (86%) and relatively weakest among the leaders of the nonbusiness interest groups (59%). No Frenchman named Germany as a threat to France, but 5% named the United States; this minority rose to 15% among the French intellectuals. A minority of this size once again suggested a possibility significant difference between the current attitudes of French and German intellectuals toward the United States, and perhaps also a difference in earlier United States policies toward the intellectuals of those two countries.

In West Germany, a threat from the Communist countries was perceived most strongly by the military (93%), civil servants (88%), and businessmen (78%), and least strongly by the university professors

44

(43%) and politicians (66%). Only one single German—a business-man—named the United States as a threat, but a minority of 8% of all respondents said that the greatest threat to German security was Germany itself—either West Germany (5%), or divided Germany (3%); and the fear of West Germany itself as a threat rose to 29% among the German university professors.[Q. 62, by occupation]

The unpopularity among French and German elites of plans for regional relaxation or arms reduction in Central Europe appears clearly in their attitudes toward the proposed denuclearization of Central Europe, which was backed only by 25% of the articulate French and 29% of the articulate German respondents. In Germany, this proposal found majority support only among the university professors (52%), and substantial minority support among the mass media personnel (43%) and the Junior Elite (31%). It was rejected as useless or worse by majorities in all groups except the university professors, and most emphatically so by the military (93%), and the civil servants (76%).[Q. 91, by age and occupation]

Despite the perception of a Communist threat, European integration was seen as primarily nonmilitary in purpose. The Communist threat was perceived as chiefly military in nature in 59% of the French responses, but only by 46% of the 134 German elite members who gave their views on this matter.[Q. 63] Strengthening the West against Communism, however, was seen as the "primary value" of European integration in only 19% of the French and 10% of the German responses to this question. In contrast, 45% of French and 67% of German responses emphasized economic and cultural purposes of European integration, and another 35% of French and 22% of German views stressed the purpose of enhancing Europe's political and diplomatic bargaining power.

The nature of the chief threat to their country, which had meant a Communist threat to 76% of all French and 70% of all German respondents,[Q. 62] was defined as "military" by 67% of the 132 French leaders who commented on this question (and 20 of whom named two threats apiece). However, their view was shared only by 46% of the 134 articulate Germans (who in more orderly fashion named only one threat each). Another 40% of German answers referred to nonmilitary Communist threats of a political, ideological, or social nature—a fear that was echoed in a negligible 3% of the French answers. French and German leaders thus in part seemed to see themselves as facing two different kinds of Communist threat. They agree on one point, however: not a single German, and only two Frenchmen, expressed any fear of Communist economic competition.[Q. 63]

Fear of a Communist military threat was stronger in both France and Germany among the Mid-Elite than among either the younger or the older leaders. A minority of 16% of the answers given by the French Junior Elite denied that there was any threat of any kind, but not a single German leader of any age appeared to share this optimism.[Q.63, by age] In France, the businessmen (78%) and the military (75%) were most insistent on seeing the Communist threat in military terms, but their view was shared by lesser but still substantial majorities among the politicians (69%) and the civil servants (59%). Only among nonbusiness groups (38%) and intellectuals (46%) did it remain a minority view. In West Germany, by contrast, majorities of the military (54%) and the businessmen (52%) emphasized the nonmilitary versions of the Communist threat. Only among the mass media personnel (67%) and the civil servants (60%) did the image of a Communist military challenge find majority support, remaining least popular among university professors (21%) and politicians (40%).[Q.63, by occupation]

The appeal of anti-Communism as a primary purpose for European integration declined in France among the younger leaders. It was endorsed by 27% of the Senior Elite, but only 18% of the Mid-Elite and 16% of the Junior Elite. In West Germany, anti-Communism as a primary European goal was least unpopular among the Mid-Elite, where 11% backed it, but it was limited to no more than 5% among both the Senior and Junior Elites.[Q.52, by age]

Among occupational elites, the military in both Germany and France furnished the strong minority support for anti-Communism as a primary European task (29% in each country). However, in France they were outdone in this respect by the political elite (35%). Economic and cultural tasks for European integration drew most support from German businessmen (79%) and university professors (76%). In France, these goals appealed most to civil servants and nonbusiness interest groups (53% each). Strengthening the political power of Europe was not a popular goal in either country, but seemed most attractive to French intellectuals (43%) and to the German military (29%).[Q.52, by occupation]

COMMON EXPECTATIONS OF GREATER FRIENDLINESS WITH EASTERN EUROPE

There was overwhelming consensus among both French and German elite members that in the next few years relations between their nations and the countries of Eastern Europe would become more cordial. Of the 118 French respondents who stated their views on this point, 99%

expected this, and they were joined in this by 83% of the 162 German elite members who answered the same question.[Q.45]   These majorities are close to constituting a record in elite opinion surveys on topics of this kind—particularly so in the case of France.   A plurality of French respondents (48%) foresaw more cordial cultural relations, while a German plurality (38%) expected greater cordiality in politics.

In France, the 99% majority comprises all differences of age and occupation.   In West Germany, more cordial relations with the countries of Eastern Europe are expected most widely among the non-business interest groups—that is, churches, farm groups, and labor unions (93%)—and, interestingly enough, among the military (92%), followed by the politicians (89%) and the Junior Elite (86%).   The relatively least optimistic group are the German mass media leaders, among whom only 70% expect more cordiality with Eastern Europe during the next years.[Q.45 by age and occupation]

MISGIVINGS ABOUT PROPOSALS FOR GERMAN CONCESSIONS

In regard to the boundaries and unity of Germany, however, the usual proposals for the relaxation of tensions were viewed with much less favor.   A bare majority—52%—of the 155 articulate German respondents to this question said that German recognition of the Oder-Neisse boundary with Poland would ease tensions in Central Europe, but they were backed only by a plurality of 42% among the 52 French elite members who cared to comment on the matter.[Q.44]   A plurality of 41% among the 153 German leaders who expressed their views also thought that recognition of the Oder-Neisse line might help German reunification, but they were supported by no more than 16% of the 50 Frenchmen who gave their views.[Q.43]   Proposals for the recognition of East Germany were viewed as still less promising.   Only 25% of 153 articulate Germans and 18% of 55 articulate French leaders thought that it might ease international tensions.[Q.42]

The German Junior Elite was even less optimistic than the older groups about the possible effects of a West German recognition of the East German regime: only 18% of the younger leaders—against 27 and 30% among the Mid-Elite and Senior Elite, respectively—thought that it might at least aid German reunification somewhat.[Q.42, by age]   The members of the Junior Elite were more optimistic than their elders, however, about the possible effects of a recognition of the Oder-Neisse line: 47% of them thought that this might be at least some help to German reunification (against only 39 and 40%, respectively, at the

Mid-Elite and Senior age levels); and 53 per cent of the Junior Elite, just as of the Mid-Elite, thought that recognizing the Oder-Neisse line might do at least some good toward easing tensions in Central Europe (against only 49% who thought so among the Senior Elite).

Among the French, this picture was reversed: their Junior Elite expected far less from any recognition of the Oder-Neisse line than did the older groups. Only 29% of the French Junior Elite favored recognition of the Oder-Neisse boundary, against 36% of the Mid-Elite and 54% of French leaders over 60 years. Only 8% of the French Senior Elite saw any use in recognizing East Germany, compared to 23% of the Mid-Elite and 16% of the younger leaders.[Q.42, 43, and 44, by age] The younger French and German leaders may find it even harder to reach agreement on some of these matters than did the older generation.

In Germany, the most hopeful occupational groups in regard to easing tensions in Central Europe through recognizing the Oder-Neisse line are the university professors (86%) and the businessmen (59%). Most opposed to this policy, considering it useless or likely to increase tensions, are the politicians (58%), the civil servants (53%), the military (50%), and the nonbusiness interest groups (50%). In France, optimism about the benefits of an Oder-Neisse recognition are greatest among the nonbusiness interest groups. Pessimism and opposition are strongest among the French military (80%) and the politicians (63%).[Q.44, by occupation]

The Communist-dominated regime of East Germany is viewed with far more misgivings than the Oder-Neisse boundary. In France, three-quarters of the articulate respondents oppose East German recognition as unhelpful or dangerous. This opposition is strong in all groups but rises to 100% of the military, 92% of the politicians, and 80% of the businessmen. In West Germany, the average opposition to recognizing the East German regime rises from 61% to 82% among the politicians, 75% among the military, and 71% among the civil servants. The optimistic minorities who hold that such recognition would ease international tensions are relatively strongest among the West German university professors (43%), media leaders (42%), and businessmen (30%).[Q.42, by occupation]

OPPOSITION TO ARMS REDUCTION FOR
CENTRAL EUROPE ONLY

The unpopularity among French and German elites of plans for regional relaxation or arms reduction in Central Europe alone appears clearly in their attitudes toward the proposed denuclearization of Central Europe, which is backed by only 25% of the articulate French and 29% of the articulate German respondents. In Germany, this proposal finds majority support only among the university professors (52%), and substantial minority support among the mass media personnel (43%) and the Junior Elite (31%). It is rejected as useless or worse by majorities in all groups except the university professors, and most emphatically so by the military (93%) and the civil servants (76%). Even among the 34 Social Democrats among our sample, only five (15%) favor the complete neutralization of Central Europe and seven (21%) favor it conditionally, but 21 (62%) wholeheartedly oppose the idea.Q.91, by age, occupation, party

French and German elite groups produced parallel majorities in six of ten questions relating to the cold war complex. But even where their overt views agreed, there were strong differences on important points and perhaps also in underlying expectations. A majority of German respondents endorsed in effect a partial continuation of the "hard line" policy of Bonn in hope that it would lead to a shift in the desirable power balance in a bipolar world, and eventually to German reunification. Many of the French respondents, on the other hand, who endorsed the same "hard line" policy, expected it to produce no particular change, but rather to preserve in an increasingly multipolar world the present German *status quo*.

Any major new armaments which either France or Germany might acquire are most likely to be used by the leaders of each country in the service of very different images of reality, of national danger, and of national interest. For the time being, however, these differences take second place, in the minds of both elites and masses, to a common fear of the spread of nuclear weapons and a common desire for their control.

5

The Common Fear of Nuclear Proliferation and the General Support for Disarmament and Arms Control

THE GREAT MAJORITY OF FRENCH AND GERMAN ELITE see themselves as realists in political and military matters. Majorities of 56% of all respondents in each country are rated by interviewers as more "tough-minded" than average in matters of foreign policy.[Q.11, b-2, Latent Attitude Survey]

As reported earlier, a Communist military threat was perceived by 59% of the articulate respondents in France, and by 46% in Germany.[Q.63] However, although inspection arrangements as part of any East-West arms control agreement are important to the Germans, they matter little to the French. They are demanded or desired by 78% of the 163 German elite members who expressed their views on this point, but this view is backed only by 38% of the 99 leaders who commented on this topic in France.[Q.94]

On-site inspections are demanded by nearly one-half of the 160 German leaders who went into particulars; and nearly one-fifth asked for aerial inspection. The 50 French leaders who commented are noncommittal: more than three-quarters say "don't know," or "leave it to the experts."[Q.95]

The German age group most insistent on inspection is the mid-elite (86%), but among the French it is the most indifferent age group on this issue (20%), showing here a French-German difference of 66 per-

50

centage points. The distance between France and Germany on this issue is least for the Senior Elites, with only 27 percentage points (70% versus 43%), and intermediate, with 33 percentage points, between the Junior Elites (76% versus 43%). Since the next five to ten years are likely to see a considerable dwindling influence of the present-day members of the Senior Elite, but little decline in the power of the members of the present Mid-Elite, French-German differences on the issue of inspection seem somewhat more likely to increase than to diminish during this short-run period, but to become perhaps more moderate as the 1970s progress.[Q.94, by age]

In West Germany, where inspection is highly popular among the 163 articulate respondents (78% insist on it, and only 7% proclaim themselves ignorant or indifferent), it is most firmly backed by business leaders (92%) and backed least by civil servants, who are the only group to give it minority support (44%). A larger proportion of the civil servants than of any other German elite group endorse inspection only conditionally (25%) or declare themselves indifferent or ignorant (13%). Of the 99 articulate French leaders, nearly one-half takes this position, and in three groups—the military (60%), the businessmen (56%), and the intellectuals (52%)—ignorance or indifference concerning inspection is professed by a majority. The strongest French minorities in favor of inspection appear among the nonbusiness interest groups (47%) and the businessmen (44%); the strongest conditional minority support to inspection is offered by the politicans (24%, as against 13% for all articulate respondents.[Q.94, by occupations]

CONSENSUS AGAINST NUCLEAR PROLIFERATION

Among the French and German elites, support for arms control and disarmament produces a striking number of strong and parallel majorities. Efforts to stop the proliferation of nuclear weapons "to countries that do not now possess them" are supported by articulate majorities of 78% in France (132 respondents) and 90% in Germany (170 respondents.[Q.79] Discussions of disarmament are favored as a means to ease international tensions by 69% of the 125 articulate French respondents and 76% of their 170 German counterparts; 20% of the French supporters of disarmament discussions, however, say that the idea is utopian but worth discussing anyway.[Q.98] A more specific plan for arms control is endorsed by 65% of 173 French and 60% of 191 German responses, and only 17 and 30% of the responses, respectively, favor no plans.[Q.90][1]   The hard core of minority opposition to arms control and disarmament comes from 30% of the articulate French respondents, but from only 9% of their German counterparts, who have heard of arms control proposals, but like none of them.[Q.89 and Q.90, cross-tabulated]

The 1963 U.S.–U.S.S.R. nuclear test ban treaty, which France had not joined, was endorsed by only 46% of the French respondents, but by 84% of those in Germany.[Q.84]   Conditional support for the test ban is equal in size—9%—but unequal in importance in the two countries. In Germany this support adds a fringe to an existing solid consensus, bringing to 93% the volume of at least conditional elite support for the test ban.   In France, it turns a plurality of test ban backers into a 55% majority for at least conditional support.[Q.84]

When asked, "Which countries, in your view, should possess nuclear weapons?"   90% of the 136 articulate French leaders and 82% of the 154 articulate German elite wanted to see such weapons restricted to those countries that currently possessed them, or to a smaller number, or to none, if possible.   Only 5% in Germany and 4% in France named Germany as a desirable possessor of nuclear arms.[Q.80]   Consensus on opposing proliferation of nuclear weapons "to countries that do not now possess them"—including Germany—is so large as to obliterate most differences between groups within each country.[Q.79]   The broader topic of the value of disarmament discussions offers somewhat better data for analysis.[Q.81]

Disarmament discussions are not a salient topic to the French elite, of whom only 125 commented on their desirability; French percentages, given below, refer only to this articulate group.   Such discussions, however, are highly salient to the German leaders, of whom 170 respondents had specific opinions; the German data below are percentages of this total group, the three who did not regard them as desirable being put into the otherwise empty "don't know" category.   Disarmament discussions receive greatest support from French nonbusiness interest groups (67%), intellectuals (54%), and politicians (54%), and least from the military (17%), the businessmen (39%), and the civil servants (39%).   The additional numbers of those who think disarmament utopian, but its discussion desirable, produce majorities among all groups, which again are largest among nonbusiness interest groups (84%), intellectuals (73%), and politicians (69%), and smallest among businessmen (54%), civil servants (64%), and the military (67%).

[1] The 173 French responses came from 124, the 191 German responses from 160 respondents, respectively.

In Germany, disarmament has definite majority support in all elite groups. It seems most worth discussing to the university professors (86%), the nonbusiness interest groups (85%), the Junior Elite (82%), and the businessmen (78%), and it won the relatively smallest majority support among the civil servants (56%) and the military (64%). Minorities rejecting disarmament discussions as utopian (and, presumably, useless or worse) are largest among French businessmen and civil servants (23% and 21%, respectively, against an 18% average for all articulate respondents), and among German civil servants and the Mid-Elite age group (38% and 19%, respectively, against a 13% average of all German respondents).$^{Q.98,}$ by age and occupation

Approval of the American-Soviet nuclear test ban treaty follows a similar pattern. Among the 136 articulate French leaders, clear-cut support is highest among French intellectuals (67%) and nonbusiness interest groups (63%), and lowest among the military (14%) and the businessmen (24%). Among the 167 German leaders who put themselves on record, definite support for the test ban is strongest among businessmen (94%, and 100% if one adds conditional supporters) and among university professors (91%), but even the lowest majorities— those among the military and nonbusiness interest groups—still show consensus at the 77% level. All kinds of disapproval of the test ban are negligible in every German group.$^{Q.84,}$ by occupation

ELITE AND MASS SUPPORT FOR FURTHER
AMERICAN-SOVIET AGREEMENTS

Further arms control and disarmament agreements between the United States and the Soviet Union are definitely backed by 52% of the 134 French and again by 84% of the 165 German respondents who commented on the matter.$^{Q.86}$ Even if their own countries should not be consulted about future arms control agreements, 55% of the 129 French respondents and 65% of the 152 Germans are still willing to support them.$^{Q.88}$

Such further arms control agreements are most strongly endorsed by German leaders of nonbusiness interest groups (96%) but almost equally strongly by German businessmen (94%) and university professors (91%). Support is weakest among the German military (42%) —the only group to give minority support on this issue—and the civil servants (63%).$^{Q.86,}$ Germany, by occupation

This general support for further American-Soviet arms control and disarmament agreements contrasts with the opposition of strong French

and German elite majorities against specific proposals for denuclearization or troop withdrawals, limited to Central Europe. It seems that
elite majorities in France and Germany see arms control and disarmament as worldwide problems, and that they would welcome steps
toward their alleviation or settlement through further agreements between the two main world powers, the United States and the Soviet
Union. At the same time they do not favor, it appears, any purely
regional agreements for Central Europe which might leave that region
a military vacuum in a heavily armed world.

This interpretation seems confirmed by the replies of 124 French and
160 German leaders to the question "Which of the various arms control
and disarmament plans do you favor?" Nonlocal plans are favored in
50% of the French replies and in 42% of the German ones, but plans
focused on Central Europe receive only 6% of the French and 16%
of the German mentions. Another 10% of the French and 3% of
the German replies endorse "any and all plans," so that the total share
of even indirect endorsements for Central European plans remains at
16% in France and 19% in Germany.[Q.90 2] The recent United States
policy of emphasizing worldwide agreements on arms control and
disarmament seems well in accord with these preferences of the French
and German elites.

If their own country should not be consulted, national pride is apt to
reduce the majorities in favor of further arms control agreements, but
with only minor changes in the ranking of the groups. The German
businessmen alone do not seem to be influenced by such considerations:
their support of arms control continues unchanged by a near-unanimous
94% majority. (Adding the conditional supporters, German business
backing for further American-Soviet arms control agreements becomes
unanimous.) Nonbusiness interest groups (74%) and university professors (65%) also remain relatively high in their support for arms
control, but at somewhat reduced levels, and the low levels of support
among the military (22%) and the civil servants (40%) become still
lower.[Q.88, Germany, by occupation]

French and German mass opinion is in striking agreement on these
points. In the summer of 1964, standard samples of voters in France
and Germany endorsed "the relaxation of tensions between the East
and the West" as good for their own country. There were solid
majorities of between 72 and 74% in both countries.[3]

On the same occasion, an American-Soviet agreement on arms limita-

---

[2] Percentages are of total mentions, since some respondents in each country
endorsed more than one plan.
[3] IFOP, EMNID, and IFAS polls, Summer 1964.

tion was definitely endorsed by 80% of 1,833 respondents in a German mass opinion poll, and rejected by only 8%. In two follow-up questions, respondents were asked first, whether they thought it possible that such an American-Soviet agreement could be reached without consulting Germany, and, second, whether this would be "bad" or "not so bad" for Germany. The slight to German national pride implied in not consulting Germany increased outright opposition to approval from the previous 8% to 13%. On the approval side, 32% of the respondents considered such an outcome possible and not so bad for Germany. Another 24% considered such an outcome impossible and thus were not asked to evaluate it, and the remaining 31% did not say or did not know. Altogether, only 45% of the original sample thus took sides on this issue, but of those who did, 71% backed further American-Soviet arms control agreement, even if Germany were not consulted. The whole sequence of responses suggests that it would be important to associate explicit German support to any American-Soviet arms control agreement, but that, in the absence of such an official consultation or association, explicit German opposition would be confined to a minority and would be balanced by an approving group of approximately equal or larger size.[4]

THE GAP BETWEEN ELITE CONCERN AND
SENSE OF INFLUENCE

The respondents in both countries had been selected in accordance with their positions of influence and their reputation as leaders or influential persons. Yet an analysis of the "Latent Attitude" Reports from the elite interviewers reveals that their own perception of their influence varies sharply between countries and in regard to different fields. Generally, Frenchmen see themselves as having less influence than do Germans. This French-German difference appears in regard to all topics, but it is strongest in matters touching upon arms control, European integration, and national foreign policy.

Furthermore, in both France and Germany, elite members see themselves most often as influential in domestic matters and in general policy decisions, but far less often in foreign policy, and least often in matters concerning either European integration or arms control. In regard to these last two topics, a sense of alienation and powerlessness seems to prevail. At the same time, there persists a sense of emotional

[4] Institut fur Angewandte Sozialwissenschaft (IFAS), Bad Godesberg, Germany. Letter of August 4, 1964.

TABLE 5-1
Emotional Intensity, Involvement, and Sense of Actual Influence Among Elite Members in France and Germany, 1964

Problem Area	Level of Affect (LAD, Q.5)			Sense of Involvement (Saliency) (LAD, Q.6)			Sense of Actual Influence (LAD, Q.4)			Lag of High Sense of Influence behind	
										Affect	Involvement
	High	Average	Low	High	Average	Low	High	Average	Low	(1 minus 7)	(4 minus 7)
	1	2	3	4	5	6	7	8	9	10	11
A. France											
1. Domestic politics	77	14	6	81	14	2	37	30	25	−40	−44
2. General policy	76	13	6	63	21	2	30	36	26	−46	−33
3. Foreign policy	79	12	6	79	16	3	17	42	33	−62	−62
4. European integration	64	23	13	63	22	10	13	39	38	−54	−53
5. Arms control	25	16	47	22	12	49	5	12	60	−20	−17
B. Germany											
1. Domestic politics	79	14	7	90	5	4	43	9	6	−36	−47
2. General policy	79	10	9	86	6	3	42	9	8	−37	−44
3. Foreign policy	87	9	5	91	4	3	38	12	7	−49	−53
4. European integration	78	15	5	90	5	3	35	16	6	−43	−55
5. Arms control	63	20	14	69	12	18	15	22	18	−48	−54

The data in this table summarize the responses to Questions 4–6 in the Latent Attitude Section I (LAD I), in our French and German elite survey, as given in our codebook. There they are coded in a seven-step code, showing differences in intensity with an eighth position for respondents whose relevant attitudes for some reason were not ascertained. The latter cases are not included in the summary table here, and they account, together with rounding errors, for the difference between 100 and the sum of the percentages of respondents rated, respectively, "High," "Average," and "Low" on each latent attitude and class of issues.

56

involvement in these topics, and an awareness of their saliency. Considerable numbers of French and German elite members thus seem seriously concerned about European integration and about arms control but feel powerless in regard to them. The distribution of these attitudes among respondents is shown in Table 5-1.

These personal feelings of powerlessness contrast with the optimistic public accounts of the progress of European integration, and with the many expressions of concern or need for arms control, all of which have appeared frequently in the public media and dicussions in the Western countries. Nonetheless, this widespread sense of lack of influence should have been expected on the grounds of at least one line of reasoning. Both arms control and European integration are parts of the possible performance of international rather than national political systems. They are processes that cannot be directed by the national instrumentalities of any single country, and they are indeed to a large extent beyond the control of any national elite. No matter how powerful elite members may be in relation to national policies in general, they are often likely to find themselves unable to shape events in these supranational fields; and it is this frequent actual lack of effective influence that confirms and reinforces, or is reflected in, the feelings of many of the French and German elite respondents.

6

Who Wants the MLF: The Lack of Support for National Nuclear Deterrents

THE IDEA OF A NATIONAL NUCLEAR DETERRENT is unpopular among the elites in France, where it is official government policy, and still more unpopular among the elites in Germany, where it sometimes has been described—by outside observers—as a significant latent aspiration. According to present evidence, it is nothing of the sort.

NATIONAL DETERRENTS SEEN AS NEITHER NECESSARY NOR CREDIBLE

A national nuclear deterrent is unnecessary for national prestige, say 63% of the 126 French respondents to this question and as many as 94% of the 166 German elite respondents.[Q.70] Nor is a national deterrent any prerequisite for national independence, according to majorities of the articulate 141 French (54%) and 171 German leaders (84%).[Q.67] Nor indeed would a national deterrent be credible to the country's enemies, in the view of 56% of the 135 French and 64% of the 101 German elite respondents recorded on this topic.[Q.72]

In France, the rejection of a national deterrent is strongest among the Senior and Junior Elites, who agree here fairly closely, and is slightly weaker among the Mid-Elite. Among the Senior and Junior Elites, 64 and 63%, respectively, opposed to 54% among the Mid-Elite, reject the national deterrent's importance for prestige; 53 and 57%, respectively, compared to 47% among the Mid-Elite, reject it as unnec-

58

essary for national independence; and 59 and 57%, respectively, among the older and younger leaders, and 47% among the middle group, reject the national deterrent as not credible to the nation's enemies.

In West Germany rejection is stronger than in France in all age groups, but often increases still more with age. The younger West German leaders are unanimous in rejecting a national nuclear deterrent as useless for national prestige. Yet while 77% of them reject a national deterrent as unnecessary also for national independence, they are exceeded at this point by the Senior (86%) and mid-elite (83%). A bare majority of 52% of the younger German leaders, as opposed to 68 and 64% of the Senior and Mid-Elite, believe that a national nuclear deterrent would not be credible to Germany's enemies, whereas 40% of the Junior Elite say that it would be credible.[Q.67, 70, and 72, by age]

In France, the strongest belief in the national deterrent as a source of prestige is shown by the military (83%), the politicians, and businessmen (54 and 40%, respectively, against an all-elite average of 34%). The support for this belief in the first two corresponding German groups is zero; it is 6% among German businessmen, and the average for all 166 articulate German respondents is 4%, with the civil servants producing the relatively largest minority in support, 19%.[Q.70, by occupations]

Beliefs in the national deterrent as a condition of independence are also strongest in France among the military (57%), the politicians (53%), and the businessmen (50%), against an average of 43% for all French elites. In Germany, this belief, explicitly rejected by 83%, is endorsed by no more than 15% of all respondents; and this share reaches its peak among the military (29%) and the civil servants (25%).[Q.67, by occupations]

The credibility of national deterrent to the enemies of France is assumed by only 34% of the 135 articulate French leaders, but among a small group of the French military this share rises to a unique and somewhat touching 86%—suggesting a remarkable gap between military and civilian perspectives in this matter—and they are followed to a far more limited extent by the French businessmen (40%). In Germany, where an average minority of 31% of 101 articulate respondents hold that a national deterrent would be credible, this view is backed most strongly by politicians (46%) and civil servants (36%). It is explicitly rejected by an average of 63%, and most emphatically by the German university professors (80%), the non-business interest groups (75%), and, interestingly enough, by the German military (71%).

Although a national deterrent thus appeals to sizable minorities among the French elites, it is at present highly unpopular, on many grounds, among the German leaders.

A LATENT FRENCH-GERMAN CONFLICT OVER NATIONAL DETERRENTS

Large French elite majorities oppose a national nuclear deterrent for Germany, and large German elite majorities oppose such a deterrent for France.   The French leaders are nearly unanimous in denying that a national nuclear deterrent is at all necessary for the independence of Germany: only 2% of the 123 articulate respondents call it necessary, and an overwhelming 93% say "no."[Q.68]   Among all German elite members, a somewhat larger minority—17%—admit that France might need a national nuclear deterrent to maintain her independence, but 76% explicitly deny this.[Q.69]

French sympathies for a German national nuclear deterrent are insignificant in all groups.   German support for a French national deterrent is lowest among businessmen (8%) but rises to 29 and 25%, respectively, among the German military and the civil servants, indicating perhaps something of the size and location of possible German Gaullist minority sentiments.[Q.68, 69, by occupation]

If these attitudes in both countries persist, any major moves toward creating or strengthening a national nuclear deterrent in either country would be likely to increase the salience of these latent disagreements between them.

PROSPECTS FOR THE FORCE DE FRAPPE

France's current national *force de frappe* is not expected to survive President de Gaulle.   Only 24% of 135 articulate French respondents expect it to be kept and strengthened, while 52% expect it to be turned into a supranational (probably European) institution, and another 7% expect it to be abandoned.[Q.73]   Sentiment in favor of keeping and strengthening the *force de frappe* after President de Gaulle's departure from the political scene is strongest among the French military (57%) and the businessmen (47%).   Turning it into a supranational force is most popular among nonbusiness interest groups (65%), intellectuals (60%), and civil servants (57%).   The small minority of those expecting the *force de frappe* to be abandoned is relatively largest among the politicians (14%).[Q.73, by occupation]

If President de Gaulle and his *force de frappe* should disappear, 25%
of 118 articulate German leaders say this would help Germany, 7%
think it would hurt her, and 48% say it would make no difference.[Q.74]
This expectation of benefits from the departure of de Gaulle and of
the *force de frappe* is strongest among West German politicians (41%).
Differentiated with respect to age, it is strongest among the German
Senior Elite (32%), less so among the Mid-Elite (26%), and least so
among the Junior Elite (13%). The opposite holds for indifference
toward de Gaulle and the *force de frappe*. The belief that their
departure would have no effect on Germany is held by 44% of the
German Senior Elite, 46% of the Mid-Elite, and 60% of the Junior
Elite.[Q.74, by age and occupation]

NATIONAL DETERRENTS JUDGED AGAINST THEIR
COSTS: THE OVERWHELMING GERMAN NEGATIVE

Although clear majorities reject the main arguments in favor of a
national nuclear deterrent, 138 articulate French respondents are
exactly divided between 46% who feel that such a deterrent is still
worth its cost, and exactly the same proportion who feel that it is not.
There is no such division in West Germany. Here the swift rejection
of a national nuclear deterrent as not worth its cost is backed by a
landslide of 95% of the 163 German respondents on this point.[Q.71]
The French military (86%) and businessmen (61%) are most in-
clined to see a national nuclear deterrent as worth its cost, and nonbusiness groups (22%) and intellectuals (36%) least so. These French
nonbusiness interest groups and intellectuals also have the greatest
tendency to reject such a deterrent as not worth the expense (67 and
52%). Among the German respondents, the huge majority rejecting
a national deterrent blurs all meaningful distinctions.[Q.71, by occupation]
These German elite data tend to invalidate the notion of a supposed
strong German desire for national nuclear weapons—a desire which
would have to be bought or headed off by offering the German Federal
Republic some share in a supranational nuclear weapons system. As
far as the evidence goes, there is no such German desire for national
nuclear weapons at this time, either on the part of the bulk of the
German elites, or on the part of German mass opinion. What interest
there is in a German national nuclear deterrent is limited to small
minorities and groups of individuals, even though some of these may
be in prominent positions.
There is no evidence that this scantiness of German popular or

elite favor for national nuclear weapons is likely to change in the near future. There is some evidence for the probable stability of trends for the next several years, and perhaps for the next decade (see Chapter 7).

DIVIDED RESPONSES TO THE MLF PROPOSAL

The proposal for a multilateral nuclear force (MLF) under NATO lacks majority support in France and Germany, and it tends to divide the elites in both countries. In France it is unqualifiedly favored by only 18%, and unqualifiedly opposed by 27% of the 100 elite respondents who commented on the proposal. In Germany, where practically all respondents commented, the same proposal divided the elites exactly, with 34% clearly in favor and an equal 34% definitely opposed.[Q.56] This last division contrasts sharply with the usual propensity for strong elite consensus in the Bonn Republic.

In view of the considerable policy interest which has attached to this issue, at least at some times, the French and German elite responses to this topic will be analyzed in somewhat greater detail.

Conditional supporters of an MLF project within NATO amount to 21% in France and 13% in Germany (as against 10 and 3% of conditional opponents, respectively). Even if all the conditions of these MLF supporters were met, the total of only conditional support would amount to 39% in France and 47% in Germany, with many respondents in the latter country volunteering the comment that they are willing to support the MLF project chiefly because it appears to be desired by the United States.[Q.56]

According to age groups, the proposed MLF under NATO is least popular among the Junior and Middle Elites in France, and the Senior and Middle Elites in Germany. Only among the French Senior Elite—the leaders over 60 years of age—does the MLF project under NATO appear potentially acceptable. Yet only 23% of this group endorse it, with 18% clearly opposed. A majority of 59% backs it conditionally, with only 27% in opposition.

The French Junior Elite, on the contrary, definitely rejects the MLF-NATO project by a plurality of 30% against 18%, and rejects it conditionally by 44% against 34%. The French Mid-Elite is most divided: those who have definite views reject the MLF-NATO idea by minorities of 22 against 13%; but the addition of conditional supporters and opponents produces an edge in favor of conditional minority acceptance, by 35% for against 31% opposed, with another—and unusual—35% of the French Mid-Elite professing themselves to be indifferent or ignorant in this matter.Q.56, France, by age

In Germany, in contrast to France, the Junior Elite produces the relatively strongest minority (41%) in clear support of MLF under NATO, as well as the relatively strongest minority in clear-cut opposition (39%), with a slight edge for those in favor of MLF. Adding the 15% of conditional MLF supporters among the young produces a majority of 56% in at least conditional support of MLF among the German Junior Elite against the same 39% of definite opponents, since none of the Junior Elite opposition to MLF appeared to be conditional.

The German Mid-Elite is divided in a way similar to the same age group in France: among the 50 to 60-year-old leaders with definite opinions, MLF under NATO is rejected by a plurality of 34%, compared to a nearly equal minority of 31% in favor, but adding the conditional supporters and opponents to each side produces a slight plurality of 42% at least conditionally in favor of the scheme, against 39% who are at least conditionally opposed to it.

The West German Senior Elite is divided similarly to the Mid-Elite: a plurality of 32% is definitely opposed to the MLF idea under NATO, whereas only 25% are definitely in support; again however, adding conditional supporters and opponents to each side shows that 40% of the older leaders would support the plan if various conditions were met, whereas 35% of the Senior Elite would remain, at least conditionally in opposition. The absence of consensus on this issue in all German age groups, as well as between the young in France and Germany, is striking. Q.56, Germany, by age

Among French occupational groups, the strongest consensus is found in the military, who definitely reject the proposed MLF under NATO by a majority of 71%, whereas 29% would favor it conditionally, and no military man was definitely in support.

All other Franch interest groups are divided. Definite opposition to MLF under NATO predominates over definite support among French businessmen (23:8%), intellectuals (26:11%), and nonbusiness interest groups (26:16%), whereas definite support is stronger among the civil servants (32:26%) and the politicians (24:19%). Adding to each side the conditional supporters or opponents of the scheme suggests that only the French intellectuals declare themselves opposed, even under various conditions, by a plurality of 37%, against 27% at least conditionally in favor. All other groups show at least conditional pluralities in favor of MLF under NATO, but only the politicians produce an at least conditional majority of 53% in favor, compared to 43% in at least conditional opposition.^{Q.56, France, by occupation}

The cleavages among occupational elites on the MLF issue are even greater in the German Federal Republic than in France. The West German military are almost as united as their French colleagues, but in the opposite direction: 71% of the Germany military definitely favor the MLF-NATO scheme; only 14% clearly oppose it; and if conditional views are taken into account, the at least conditional support for the plan rises to 78%. Also among the West German politicians there is clear-cut majority support for the proposal: 60% definitely favor MLF under NATO, and another 11% would do so on conditions, with only 24% as definite opponents, and no conditional opponents.

The opposite consensus prevails among the German mass media elite: 67% definitely reject the MLF-NATO scheme, as opposed to only 19% clearly in favor, and another 10% in favor with conditions.

All other West German interest groups are divided with no definite majority on either side of the issue. Definite pluralities reject the scheme among the four remaining groups: the university professors (33:10%), the civil servants (25:19%), the nonbusiness interest groups (44:33%), and the businessmen (29:22%). If conditional supporters and opponents are added, the university professors (38:29%) and the businessmen (38:34%) remain in opposition, but the nonbusiness interest groups become evenly divided (48:48%), and the civil servants now produce a conditional plurality in favor (38:25%). It should be borne in mind that part of the definite support—and presumably also some of the conditional support—for the MLF-NATO proposal was given on the explicit grounds that the German leaders wanted to go along with what they consider to be a United States initiative and desire.

A PROPOSED EUROPEAN NUCLEAR FORCE:
FRENCH AND GERMAN DISAGREEMENTS

A European multilateral nuclear force, independent of NATO, would be somewhat more popular among elites in France, where a plurality of 40% of 134 respondents clearly favor it, with only 12% clearly opposed, but it would be much less popular in Germany, where no more than 6% of 168 respondents back the project, whereas a solid 80% express their clear-cut opposition.

Definite French support for such a European nuclear force is highest among the civil servants (53%) and lowest among the political leaders (23%) and the military (29%), with all others interest groups not far from the average. Adding the conditional supporters produces at least conditional majorities among all occupational groups, rising to 100% among the military.Q.82, France by occupation

In West Germany, on the contrary, a European nuclear force independent of NATO is definitely rejected by large majorities in all groups with respect to both age and occupation. This German opposition rises from two-thirds of the Junior Elite and the mass media leaders to 83 and 88% among the Mid-Elite and the Senior Elite, respectively, and to 85% of the members of nonbusiness interest groups and 95% of the German university professors. Definite support among the German elite groups for such a European nuclear force is almost negligible. Among the German age groups, it ranges from 8% of the Mid-Elite to 5% of the Junior and 4% of the Senior Elites. Among occupational groups, it ranges from 11% of the nonbusiness interest groups and 10% of the mass media leaders to none of the university professors, 3% of the businessmen, and 7% of the military. An average of only 14% of all 168 articulate German elite respondents offer the plan even conditional support. The relatively largest minorities of such conditional backers are found among civil servants (25%) and the mass media elite (24%), and there is an average level of conditional minority support among the business leaders (15%), the politicians (14%), and the military (14%).Q.82, Germany, by age and occupation

In almost every aspect of this issue, the contrast between France and Germany is unmistakable.

FRENCH-GERMAN DIVISIONS IF MLF WERE AN
ACCOMPLISHED FACT

If a multilateral nuclear force (MLF) within NATO should become an accomplished fact, much of French opposition would persist unless particular French conditions were met, but much of German elite opposition would change into support. The proportions of the various responses to these and related questions confirm an impression created by the interviews: there is no substantial German pressure for an MLF, but rather a willingness to go along with such a scheme if Germany's ally, the United States, should insist on it.

If such an MLF within NATO should come into existence, only 16% of the 102 French respondents to this question would definitely wish their country to participate, but only 9% would be definitely opposed. Among the 160 German respondents to the same question these proportions are reversed: 58% clearly would favor participation in such a NATO development once it had come into existence, and only 17% would definitely oppose it.[Q.57]

Most French views on this question, however, are conditional: 43% of the articulate French elite respondents are willing to participate in a NATO-related MLF, once it is in existence, and if their conditions were met; and another 21% announced themselves in conditional opposition, making for a total of 59% of at least conditional support against only 30% of at least conditional opposition. Making the MLF a reality within NATO, these responses suggest, would not in itself bring about French participation in it; if conditional support were to be made actual, and if French cooperation were to be assured, at least some major French conditions would have to be met. In Germany, by contrast, most views are expressed in definite terms from the outset: only 13% of conditional supporters and 5% of conditional opponents could be added to their respective sides, making not much difference to the expectable outcome.[Q.57]

The implications seem worth restating. On an earlier question, only 18% of articulate German respondents definitely favored the creation of an MLF within NATO, and only 39% favored it at least conditionally.[Q.56] With MLF in NATO assumed to be an accomplished fact, however, definite support for German participation in such a going concern rises to 58%, and at least conditional support increases to 71%.[Q.57] Only a small minority of German leaders thus shows any desire to initiate or ask for the creation of a multilateral nuclear force within NATO, but a majority does not wish to be left out should such a force come into existence.

This latter desire is somewhat weaker among the German Junior Elite, where only 54% express it in definite form, while an above-average proportion of the young (21%) indicate conditional support. Among the French, definite support for NATO-MLF, once it came into existence, would be negligible for the Mid-Elite (4%), slightly below average for the Junior Elite (14%), and appreciable only for the Senior Elite (28%). In regard to conditional support, the French Junior Elite is slightly above average (43%), and it includes the relatively largest minority in definite opposition (14%). If there should be no other major changes, the gradual retirement of the Senior Elite by 1970–1975 would leave the French elites slightly more opposed to participation in a NATO-linked MLF than they are today, but it would very slightly increase sympathies for such participation among the German leaders, and would thus somewhat increase the existing policy differences between the two countries in this matter.[Q.57, by age]

Among French occupational elites, definite support for participating in a once-established MLF within NATO is largest among the civil servants (28%) and the politicians (22%), and the smallest among the military and the businessmen, where it amounts to zero in both groups. Conditional support, however, is highest among businessmen (62%) and politicians (57%), indicating at least some readiness in these two groups to contemplate a future deal with NATO, if acceptable arrangements were offered. Definite opposition is strongest among the French military (29%), and conditional opposition highest among the civil servants (44%) and again among the French military (also 29%), raising the total of at least conditional opposition among the military to 58%. Among the German interest groups, in contrast to the French, the military express the greatest definite desire to participate in an MLF within NATO, if it should come to exist (79%). They are followed in this view at some distance by the politicians (66%), with other occupational groups close to or below average. Conditional support is strongest among civil servants (31%), while definite opposition is expressed by the largest minorities among the mass media leaders (33%) and the nonbusiness interest groups (22%).

AN OPPORTUNITY FOR THE UNITED STATES

The pattern of responses to this entire complex of questions suggests that neither French nor German elites are pressing strongly at this time for nuclear weapons, either national or collective. Rather, the issues of the national deterrent and the MLF most often tend to evoke opposition or division. This contrasts with the high majorities in both countries in favor of general arms control, though not in favor of merely local arms control agreements limited to Central Europe. As far as this evidence goes, it suggests that French and German elites are currently open to broader ideas or plans for arms control, covering larger parts of the world, and that in this regard the United States has at present, in Europe, a relatively wide range of discretion and a significant opportunity for leadership.

7

Outlook for a Decade: The Stability of Trends

NEITHER THE FRENCH NOR THE GERMAN ELITES foresee any drastic
future changes in the basic attitudes and policies of their own
nations and of the major interest groups and elites within them. Nor,
indeed, do either anticipate that their own attitudes might change.
Although they know, as experienced persons must know, that many
unexpected things could happen in the next ten years, and that a great
many changes could occur, the interviews leave the impression that
these French and German leaders are less concerned with the possibility of major future changes than would be their counterparts in the
United States.

Some of the French and German elite expectations of basic continuity
in their main national policies, attitudes, and institutions have been
reported in Chapter 2. Another set of indications on this topic comes
from age group analysis of respondents and responses.

THE EVIDENCE FROM AGE GROUP ANALYSIS

As far as the evidence from the analysis of age groups goes, the
prospects for the next ten years may be none too different. An
analysis of French responses by age group shows no major or consistent
differences in attitudes revealed. On all questions, age accounts for
less than 10% of the variance observed, and on only one question,
answered by only about one-third of the respondents, does age account
for more than 5% of the outcome.[1]

[1] The source for this statement is Tau B tests on cross-tabulations of age cohorts

Within these limits, the most significant differences on 11 key questions in France are those between the French Mid-Elite, on the one hand, and both the Senior Elites and the Junior Ascending Elites, on the other. The Mid-Elite, composed of respondents born between 1904 and 1914, is the generation whose members were on the average about 20 years old in 1939, and who thus were in all likelihood most profoundly formed in their outlook by the experiences of the 1930s and of the Second Word War, including the collapse of France, the Nazi occupation and the French resistance, the 1944 liberation, and the first de Gaulle regime. As regards specific questions, elite members from this intermediate age group give the strongest unqualified endorsement to the de Gaulle regime (38%), against only 17 and 25% from the Senior and Junior elites, respectively—and the addition of those moderately satisfied brings to 59% the Mid-Elites who give at least qualified support to the regime.[Q.1, by age]

The leaders in their fifties also are most nearly unanimous (94%) in perceiving current French policies as increasingly nationalistic in flavor, and nearly two-thirds of them—65%—as opposed to 55% among their seniors and only 47% among the youngest leaders—assert a "manifest destiny" for France. The same middle elite age group includes the strongest minorities who favor independent national action in foreign policy, and who believe that the old parties are dead. This latter belief soon proved to be unrealistic, to judge from the March, 1965 municipal elections and the December, 1965 presidential elections.[Q.8 & 27] The identification of this middle elite group with the de Gaulle regime carries over into foreign policy: 44% expressed their enthusiastic approval, whereas only 27% among their seniors and 31% among the younger leaders did.[Q.31, by age] The addition of those who are mildly approving brings the total of at least mild support for current French foreign policies to over two-thirds among the middle group, compared to a minority of only 47% among the older men and a bare majority of 51% among the younger group.[2]

---

with the interview questions.[52.1] (For a discussion of the Tau B test, see H. Blalock, Jr., *Social Statistics* (New York, McGraw-Hill, 1960), pp. 232–234; cf. also Goodman and Kruskal's "Tau B," *ibid.*) The relevant French elite interview questions found ranking relatively high on this test, in relation to age cohorts, are questions No. 1, 8, 27, 31, 37, 42, 44, 46, and 47. The analysis of the responses to questions 42, 43, and 44 should be treated with particular caution, however, since these questions had only 55, 50, and 52 articulate respondents, respectively, comprising little more than one-third of our sample.

[2] The contrast between the strong Gaullist identification among the elite age group in their fifties and the relative skepticism of their elders may not be paralleled on the level of mass opinion, where the greatest support for General

Not surprisingly, the French Mid-Elite is also the age group which seems to be least friendly to Germany. It includes the strongest minority that is flatly against German reunification (29%), and a majority of 54% oppose it at least conditionally. In this respect, they differ somewhat from their elders, but are matched very nearly by their juniors. The Mid-Elite also includes the relatively largest majority, 23%, who think that diplomatic recognition of East Germany might ease international tensions, whereas 15% say that such recognition would make tensions worse, and 54% feel that it would make no difference. Among their juniors, only 16% favor recognition of East Germany, and a group twice as large, 32%, oppose it as leading to more conflict, whereas only 40% think it would have no effect.

On most of the issues mentioned, the French Junior Elite occupy a position intermediate between the Mid-Elite and the Senior Elite group.[3] On some matters, however, the members of the Junior Elite take a distinctive position. They are the only age group to favor unconditionally, by a bare majority of 51%, further steps toward limiting national sovereignty—something only 47% of the senior group and only 32% of the Mid-Elite are willing to do. When one adds to these hardcore numbers those willing to limit national sovereignty on various conditions, the differences between the age groups almost disappears in the overall conditional majority of 83%.[Q.47, by age] The Junior Elite includes the strongest plurality—48%—who flatly favor cooperation in alliances, and the smallest group—only 8%—who definitely favor independent national foreign policy for France.[Q.27, by age]

However, the French Junior Elite is also strongest in predicting that current French policies toward the United States and NATO will continue after de Gaulle, and the Junior Elite group is still more distrustful than its elders of any proposals for recognizing the Oder-Neisse boundary between Germany and Poland—a matter concerning which most French leaders seemed to prefer to leave well enough alone—but here the limited number of articulate respondents on these questions makes the results of such cross-tabulations by age somewhat doubtful.

Among the French Senior Elite, a plurality of 38% is flatly dissatisfied with the present regime, and the addition of the conditionally dis-

---

de Gaulle was found among older voters and women. (Communication by Mme. Helene Riffault, Director, Institut Francais d'Opinion Publique, Paris, April 1965.)

[3] Of the French sample, 16% were under 40 years old and 29% were between 40 and 50, amounting to a total junior elite of 45%. The corresponding age groups among the German elite sample were 8%, 15% and 23%, respectively.

satisfied brings the total opposition, actual and conditional, among the older leaders to a majority of 55%.[Q.1, by age]   They have least admiration for the present foreign policy, and relatively most sympathies for Western Germany.[Q.31 & 33, by age]   They are most strongly in favor of further steps to limit national sovereignty: 47% want to do this unconditionally, and another 47% will join them on conditions, producing among the elderly leaders an at least conditionally internationalist total of 94%.   The passing of many leaders of this older generation from the active scene during the next five years may well make some of the tasks of United States foreign policy more difficult.

THE EXPECTATIONS OF ELITE RESPONDENTS

Elite members themselves do not expect to change their minds. Closure of thinking to a more than average extent is found among a majority of French elite respondents in regard to both domestic and foreign policy.   Although they often choose skeptical or conditional alternatives in reply to a particular question, 72% quite clearly expect that the methods proposed by them for defending the French national interest—whatever these methods might be—most probably will continue to be feasible in the future, and only 1% think that the methods proposed now might become impracticable at some future time.[Q.29]

Definite expression of such closure of thinking is noted most often among the French military (86%) and the civil servants (79%), but they constitute a majority even of the relatively least closed-minded of the French groups, the intellectuals (58%).[Q.29, by occupation]

A brief follow-up survey by mail was conducted in December 1964 among the same group of French elite respondents, after such conspicuous changes as President Johnson's electoral victory in the United States, Premier Khrushchev's fall in Russia, the Chinese nuclear explosion, and the French-German disputes over Common Market agriculture and the MLF.   Usable replies were received from about 60% of the respondents.   These tended to confirm the picture of the summer 1964 interviews and to show the relative stability of the underlying attitudes among French leaders.

SOME PROSPECTS FOR FRENCH POLITICS

In France, the passage of time should weaken the influence of the pro-alliance Senior Elites first, but concomitantly or shortly thereafter it should increase the influence of the equally pro-alliance younger leaders, with only limited net changes in the total balance of influence to be expected for the next five years. Only after about ten years, when perhaps one-half of the present Mid-Elite will have retired or be close to retirement, will the automatic working of time have substantially weakened the nationalistic influence of that more strongly Gaullist or quasi-Gaullist generation.

Until then, and hence for the next ten years, the large proportion of uncommitted, or only conditionally committed, leaders may be decisive. Their response to this or that international situation, or to this or that policy of the United States may yet prove most relevant for the future foreign policy of France under President de Gaulle and his successors.

At the same time, the basic French preoccupation with national self-assertion and self-reassurance is likely to remain. There is no majority consensus among the multiple responses to the question, "Which features of French foreign policy, if any, are likely to persist after de Gaulle?" but the strongest plurality—34%—forecast the continuation of the current (and none too cooperative) French policies toward the' United States and NATO, followed by 27% foreseeing a continuation of the current policy of Franco-German *rapprochement*, 15% expecting the continuation of current French policies toward the East, and 12% prophesying continuity after de Gaulle toward non-Western countries, including presumably Southeast Asia and China.[Q.33] The present French style of somewhat prickly and self-assertive diplomacy might thus be modified in form and in relatively marginal matters, but may well persist in substance.

Expectations of continuity for the present French policies toward the United States and NATO are strongest among civil servants, while support for continuing the current policies toward a French-German rapprochement and European integration is strongest among the military. A relatively strong group among the businessmen (24%) name, as likely to persist after de Gaulle, the current French policies toward "the East," i.e., primarily toward the Soviet Union and the members of its bloc in Eastern Europe. Otherwise, expectations about post-Gaullist French foreign policy are fairly evenly distributed among all groups.[Q.33, by occupation]

At the same time, this continuing French diplomacy of national self-assertion will have to be carried out after de Gaulle by relatively unstable coalition governments presiding over a persistently divided domestic political system. The interviews show the elite respondents nearly evenly divided among Gaullists, "riders" supporting Gaullist policies for temporary or opportunist reasons, "notables" continuing to represent the old pre-Gaullist political parties and interest groups of the Fourth Republic, "aspirants" clinging to the hopes for a national and republican renewal in the tradition of the French Resistance movement of the Second World War, and the unreconstructed diehards of the extreme right and extreme left.

Among all these, clear-cut Gaullists constitute less than one-fifth, and although there is majority consensus that the Fourth Republic will not be restored, and almost definite majority consensus that the Fifth Republic will survive de Gaulle in many of its major aspects and institutions, there is no agreement on just which features will survive.[Q.14] Rather, a majority see France divided by cleavages on fundamental domestic political issues and, only to a slightly lesser extent, on matters of class or ideology, such as the conflict between left and right.[Q.4 & 5] The old political parties are seen as surviving by 70% of the respondents in 1964,[Q.8 & 15] and their view is confirmed as realistic by the success of these parties in the municipal elections of March, 1965.

Gaullism thus has by no means swept the political scene or permeated the fabric of French politics, but neither is the Fifth Republic a surface affair that will vanish after President de Gaulle. If one adds to the 48% of French leaders who expect the Fifth Republic to survive de Gaulle—and more than half of them are not Gaullists—another 24% who expect it to survive under various conditions, then it becomes clear that nearly three out of four French elite respondents are more willing to bet on its survival than on its demise. Indeed, only 18% expect even conditionally that it will not survive de Gaulle. This expectation of the persistence of the Fifth Republic is strongest among businessmen—80% of them are certain that the Fifth Republic will endure, and not a single businessman gave a negative answer—and relatively weakest among the nonbusiness interest groups and the intellectuals, whereas nearly one-half of the military avoid giving an opinion.[Q.14, by occupation]

The elite interviews of 1964 show clearly that the hope for a "new politics," which would overcome those old conflicts by more pragmatic and cooperative approaches, has thus far not materialized below the surface of the personal popularity of President de Gaulle. This forecast was confirmed by the less than 16% of the popular vote which was cast in December, 1965 for the "French Kennedy," M. Jean Lecanuet, the candidate who seemed to represent most nearly this pragmatic, new, and somewhat pro-American approach.

Rather, a majority of elite members both expect and desire political changes in French domestic politics after General de Gaulle's departure, but with no clear-cut agreement on their nature. The result of this combination of persistent cleavages and divergent future expectations is most likely to be a France governed by coalition regimes of one kind or another (though probably not by a revived Popular Front, which would be opposed by a majority of elite members). French foreign and military policy after de Gaulle is thus likely to be somewhat weaker, and more divided and enmeshed in French domestic political conflicts than it is now.

Either under General de Gaulle or under his successor, therefore, French foreign policy will be more clear-cut in appearance than in substance. The French elites are unlikely to renounce the essential protection of a limited American alliance or the benefits of limited European economic cooperation. But they are no more likely to consent at any early date to merge or subordinate their country economically, militarily, or politically into any truly effective supranational system governed by the will of non-French powers or majorities. If, on the one hand, international tensions should relax, the French elites may find it easier to maintain their policy of limited sovereignty-cum-alliances. If East-West tensions should intensify, on the other hand, French leaders may support limited gestures of Western solidarity at moments of crisis—similar to President de Gaulle's announcement of support for the United States in the Cuban missile crisis of October 1962—but they may also insist on France's being treated as a substantial, autonomous power whose views on policy must be given weight, and who cannot be expected to accept the policy judgments of the United States as *ipso facto* superior to those of the other members of the Western coalition. So long as no such equalitarian coordination of American and French viewpoints appears feasible, French gestures underlining French independence are likely to recur.

On the fundamental matters of a distinct French national identity, substantial sovereignty and ever-resurgent self-assertion, the foreign policies of President de Gaulle represent many of the genuine long-term preferences of the French elites and the French people. In this general sense, President de Gaulle is truly representing France; and any power desiring French cooperation in international politics will have to bear this fact in mind.

THE PROSPECTS FOR CONTINUITY IN WEST GERMANY

It seems reasonable to be more reserved in one's judgment of the future politics of Germany, after all the startling changes of mood and politics that have occurred there during the last six decades.

Nonetheless, it must be reported that the visible indications of stability and continuity of the attitudes of the present elite of the German Federal Republic are even stronger than they are in France.   Among elite members, as well as on the level of mass opinion, as far as the attitudes surveyed in this study are concerned, the younger age groups in West Germany generally do not seem to differ greatly from their elders.   Exceptions have been indicated in earlier chapters, but, in general, age accounts for even less of the variance of elite attitudes in West Germany than in France.

Regardless of age, German leaders are even less willing than the members of the French elite to consider that the basic policies which they now favor might eventually become out of date.   An overwhelming 96% of 161 articulate German respondents to this question feel definitely that the policies which they have suggested for defending the national interest of their country will continue to be feasible in the future.   This chorus of certainty overcomes all distinctions of age and occupation.Q.29, Germany.   Only one single German respondent out of 161 denied this.

The explicit appraisals by the interviewers confirm this picture of a much higher degree of closure of the minds of the German elite respondents than of their French counterparts.   If 48% of the French leaders are rated as having closed minds to an "above average" extent, this rating applies to as many as 74% of the German elite members. On matters of foreign policy, the cloture of German elite minds seems even higher, with 79%, against 52% in France.LAD–I, Q.7, b–1 & b–2   Even in regard to arms control, where knowledge and hardened views are less frequently found, German minds seem definitely made up in 62% of the cases, as against only 31% in France—a rare and perhaps significant area of openmindedness in French elite thinking.LAD–I, Q.7, b–4   It is possible, of course, that large changes in mass or elite attitudes may be in the making, deep below the surface of French or German politics.   All that can be reported is that no evidence for any such major changes has been found in the study.

8

Prospects for Policy

BEYOND A FOUR-POWER OR FIVE-POWER AGREEMENT, with United
Nations backing, to retard or stop proliferation of nuclear
weapons to countries that do not now possess them, it might be useful
to speculate, in the light of the general impressions derived from interviews, press analyses, and other data, about the requirements of a more
effective European and Atlantic integration policy as well as European
acceptance of arms control. The reader should be warned that we are
now entering the realm of speculation. If concerned only with findings based on fact, he should stop here. If he is willing to follow some
thoughts that have been suggested by considering some of these facts,
he may take these concluding comments for whatever they may be
worth.

THE UNITED STATES INTEREST IN
WESTERN CONSENSUS

No single man has created these problems of Allied consensus on
arms control and the prevention of nuclear proliferation, or the
problems of European and Atlantic unity (or at least dependable
alliance)—neither the President of France nor the President of the
United States. Rather these are problems in part created, or at least
aggravated, by an inherent conflict among two of our own policies.
The United States is driven by its national interests to promote supranational policies for strengthening the Western alliance and for con-
trolling and containing the pace of competitive armament among the
powers. However, in perceiving and pursuing its national interests,

the United States is still acting very much like a nation-state which expects other nations to follow its decisions.

The tighter an alliance becomes, or the more closely a political community is knit, the more constraints it imposes on each of its members in their right to decide upon peace or war in the light of their own national consideration, however right and reasonable they may seem. The only way of retaining one's freedom of national decision-making about even limited war or peace, while keeping one's allies, would be to attain complete political or moral hegemony over them. The major nations of Western Europe, such as France, are not likely to concede for long this kind of hegemony to any other power. In the pursuit of Western unity, there may be no long-run substitute for consensus politics.

A more broadly integrative policy would require that France, Britain, and Germany be conceded a substantial share in Allied decision making, not only as a matter of ceremony, but also in regard to substance. Any Allied agreement on arms control, on the one hand, or any armed confrontation with some Communist power or powers, on the other hand, entails a sharing of real risks between the United States and its major allies, including France, Britain, West Germany, and, outside Europe, at least Japan. Together, these countries have a larger population than the United States, and in the aggregate, comparable geographic, industrial, and intellectual resources. As these countries have recovered from the ravages of the Second World War, their elites, as well as their masses, have become inevitably ever more disinclined to support Western policies in the making of which they have no major share.

Due to the differences in outlook and interests among these several countries, as well as between each of them and the United States, more genuinely common policies will be difficult to work out, and they will be limited in scope. The alternative of the United States' setting policy more or less unilaterally, and chiefly in the light of national American estimates of Soviet or Asian reactions—and in the light of American domestic political considerations—seems likely to erode our alliances increasingly over the next few years.

If the second of these tendencies—the tendency to unilateral policy setting by the United States—should prevail in the next few years, chronic conflicts between American policies and those of France, and perhaps of others among our allies, are likely to persist and grow. During the decade 1966–1976, such conflicts are likely to impede the reaching of any major international arms control agreements, the already strained functioning of NATO, and the already halting progress of European integration, by producing persistent cleavages between the pro-American elite majorities of West Germany and the elites of France. If, on the other hand, genuine sharing of decisions among the major Western powers should prove feasible, no spectacular gains should be expected within the next decade. Nonetheless, further important and hopeful change may be initiated. Frenchmen and Germans are getting used to the idea that wars within Western Europe are unlikely and somehow illegitimate. They are ceasing to expect them and to devote resources to their preparation.

On a world scale, it should be possible under these conditions to obtain a limited but effective agreement to extend the nuclear test ban and to slow down nuclear proliferation. During the same period it should also be possible to preserve and gradually extend the present Atlantic alliance and the "Europe of Fatherlands" now linked to a degree in the European Common Market. By doing so, it should be possible to consolidate and strengthen in the minds and economic practices of West Europeans those images and incipient habits of European unity that may offer a basis for more spectacular advances toward European integration after 1975.

THE CONTINUING PROBLEM OF FRENCH-AMERICAN RELATIONS

At this time, however, the problem of French-American relations is becoming acute. Politics is, among other things, the art of avoiding intolerable choices; but for the French elites, a choice between loss of NATO membership and persistent and conspicuous political inequality within NATO would be close to intolerable. They continue to see NATO, and even more, the United States, as the ultimate foundations of French military security. At the same time, they have not been able to avoid seeing the position of France as persistently unequal in NATO, in the Western alliance, and in the policy considerations of the United States.

For two decades, French views, French knowledge, French experiences, and French interests, as seen by the French, simply have weighed less with the United States than have the views and interests of Britain or of Germany, and they seem to have weighed far less with us than have the views of our domestic interest groups and voters. This relative disregard of French views has included areas where many members of the French elite feel that France has had—and should continue to have—particular knowledge, competence, experience, and interests. In Syria and Lebanon, in Egypt and Tunisia, in Indochina and Algeria, in Europe and the Far East, in nuclear policies and in matters of international finance: in all these matters it seems to them that French views have received relatively little consideration and respect from a variety of American administrations.

It is obvious and natural that to the French their own views appear true, rational, and realistic. Seeing French views disregarded by their allies not only hurts the pride of French leaders but also damages a broader range of their values, and ultimately challenges their perception of reality and their self-respect. The choice between relaxing or affirming their alliance with the United States thus subjects French elite members to the strain of having to choose—seemingly or actually—between heightened military insecurity or persistent and humiliating status deprivation.

There is not much the French themselves can do to escape this increasingly unacceptable dilemma, unless they can become self-sufficient in nuclear defense by acquiring a national "bee-sting" capacity, small but sufficient to inflict such severe nuclear second-strike damage upon any possible aggressor that, though France might perish, no attack on France would be attractive to any rational foreign government. Seen from this viewpoint, it becomes understandable why nearly one-half of the French leaders consider the *force de frappe* "worth its cost," although many of them explicitly doubt or deny its present necessity, credibility, or prestige value. Perhaps this also explains why there was a further shift in favor of the *force de frappe* by December, 1964. A French nuclear deterrent, even though of little value in the present, still may seem to offer to many of the French one of the few distant avenues for escaping from the painful dilemma of entrapment between their own military defenselessness and what is likely to seem to them persistent American political disdain.

It might be necessary, therefore, to take the French more fully into the nuclear club, on the understanding that a limited "bee-sting" nuclear capacity cannot be used short of the probable military suicide of the user. This fuller acceptance of France as a nuclear power could best occur within the framework of a tacit or explicit East-West agreement to limit nuclear weapons to the five powers now possessing them, and France could be further integrated into a reformed NATO structure. It is difficult to forecast the personal reaction of President de Gaulle to such a United States policy, but there is reason to think that it might be acceptable to a majority of the French elite.

A POSSIBLE POSITIVE DEVELOPMENT FOR NATO
AND ITS PRICE FOR THE UNITED STATES

A possible step in this direction of genuinely and visibly shared decision-making might be the creation of a Four-Power NATO Executive Committee, to be responsible for major matters of politics and economics, as well as security and strategy. This Executive Committee would be composed of the United States, Britain, France, and the German Federal Republic. Its chairman would ordinarily be chosen by each of the four members in rotation, but the chairman would always be furnished by one of the European members of the Committee when primarily European matters were on the agenda. Such a Four-Power NATO Executive Committee could take on many functions of a political directorate or cabinet of the Western alliance.

At the same time it might be important to emphasize the distinctive and separate control of technical questions and decisions on nuclear weaponry, long-range delivery systems, and the ABC weapons, which Germany renounced under the 1954 Paris Agreements, but which are still important to the French. Although the general competence of the Four-Power NATO Executive Committee should include broad questions of strategy, it should have at its side a separate NATO Technical Subcommittee on Nuclear Defense, composed of the three NATO members now possessing nuclear weapons, i.e., the United States, Britain, and France.

There is reason at this time to expect that such an arrangement would be acceptable to the predominant elite and mass opinion not only in France but also in the German Federal Republic. Continued German participation in the integrative work of EEC and in the new NATO Four-Power political directorate would, in all likelihood, make this acceptance permanent.

Such a policy would have its price. To give political significance to such a Four-Power Committee, all four members, including the United States, would have to bind themselves to take no substantial military action above the routine police level anywhere in the world, regardless of provocation, without the prior consent of the NATO Executive Committee. If the four powers should wish to exempt cases of utmost national emergency involving a vital national interest—a reservation the United States might well require for itself—they might have to agree to be quite sparing in invoking this exception.

For the United States, as for all other NATO powers, this would mean the renunciation of the sovereign right to initiate or escalate a war by one-sided national decision. Such a limitation already has been accepted in substance by the other NATO powers. In effect, Turkey accepted it at the time of the Cyprus crisis in the early 1960s; France and Britain did so even earlier at the end of the Suez crisis in 1956. Only the United States is now left to accept for itself the same rule of conduct which we already require from our allies.

If such an improved NATO agreement, formal or tacit, should emerge, the status of the NATO Executive Committee might soon become such that the ineradicable French—and potentially European—desire for political and symbolic equality might be in large part accommodated. Then some early progress could be made toward meeting the no less ineradicable desire of the great majorities of the peoples and elites of France and Germany, as well as of Europe, for an effective combination of security and arms control.

Public acceptance of such a rule of good citizenship in the Atlantic Alliance might increase in the future the freedom of the President of the United States to resist the warlike clamor of domestic opponents and pressure groups, if he should so desire. By thus adding an effective supranational control stage to the national decision-making process of the United States, the safety, efficiency, and reliability of American policy-making could be substantially improved.

Appendix A

TWO QUESTIONS WERE USED to divide our respondents into those with a European orientation and those with an Atlantic orientation. First, Q.55, "Do you feel that (Germany) (France) should rather endeavor to strengthen NATO, or European unity (EEC), or both?" was applied to determine the basic attitude of the respondents. Those who answered "Work primarily to strengthen NATO," were considered Atlantics, and those who answered "Work primarily to strengthen European unity (EEC)," Europeans. Respondents with negative answers, like "Work to strengthen neither," and "Work to weaken NATO," were put into the group "Neither," since their attitudes seemed to indicate that they were against any supranational orientation. Respondents who had answered "Work to strengthen both" were tested for their responses to Q. 82, "Would you favor a European nuclear force independent of NATO?" and Q. 56, "What do you think of the widely-discussed proposal of a multilateral nuclear force under NATO command?"

Since an unfavorable response to either question did not necessarily reflect an opposition of the respondent to supranational bodies, either Atlantic or European, but could just as well have been caused by a basic opposition to nuclear weapons, only a favorable answer could serve as an indication of the respondent's leaning. If the answer showed that the respondent favored either a European Nuclear Force or MLF, he was added to the Europeans or the Atlantics, respectively. If, however, the answers to both questions were favorable, this was taken as further proof that the respondent in fact favored both NATO and European unity. On the other hand, if a respondent who had answered "both" to Q. 55 failed to answer favorably either Q. 82 or Q. 56, or both, he was still considered "Pro-NATO and Pro-Europe" because of his first response to Q. 55, a question that had quite strong and clear-cut wording. As previously mentioned, opposition to MLF or a European Nuclear Force was not taken as an indication of Anti-Europe or Anti-NATO feelings.

In the same way, respondents were tested who had failed to show a definite stand on Q. 55, answering "D. K.," or whose answers were not ascertained. Their responses to Q. 82 and Q. 56 determined whether they were included with the Europeans, the Atlantics, or the group "Pro-Europe and Pro-NATO." Only if they did not give favorable answers to either of these two questions was it impossible to include them in any of the three groups, and they were added to the group "Neither." Respondents who had shown a definite orientation by their answers to Q. 55, clearly choosing either NATO or Europe, were not tested further for their responses to Q. 82 and Q. 56 because of the uncertainties in the evaluation of unfavorable answers to these questions, and, primarily, because of the stronger wording of Q. 55.

Question 98, "Do you think it is possible to ease international tension by disarmament, or is the whole question of disarmament and arms control a mere utopia not worth discussing?" was used to determine attitudes toward arms control. Those who answered "Disarmament is a utopian scheme not worth discussing" were coded as being in favor of further arms competition. The same applied to those who answered "Disarmament is worth discussing, but not at the present time," because it seemed evident from their response that at the present time they considered further competition necessary and imperative, though not desirable.

A respondent was coded as being in favor of arms control if he answered "Disarmament is definitely worth discussing (progress can be made)" and "Disarmament is utopian, but worth discussing anyway." Unlike the responses previously quoted, which considered disarmament worth discussing but not at the present time, this response was interpreted as basically for control, although the respondent believed that this end could not be achieved under present circumstances, and perhaps not at all.

A third category was provided for those with undecided or not ascertained answers.

The next step was to break down the sample according to the political status the respondent anticipated for his country. The answers to Q. 27, "Do you feel that for a nation like (Germany) (France) an independent foreign policy is outmoded, or does every nation have to act by its national interest alone, even at the expense of international cooperation?" were used to divide the sample into those favoring independent national policy and those for alliances. Those favoring alliances were broken down further according to their responses to Q. 48, "What form of union most nearly describes an integrated Europe as you generally think of it?" Those answering "International system as now, cooperation and coordination only," and "Mix system with national dominance," appear in the box "Alliance among Sovereign Nations." The respondents favoring a confederation were considered to be for partial integration. Those who thought of an integrated Europe as a mixed system with supranational dominance, a federal system, or a unitary European state, were put into the box "Political integration, all the way."

All respondents who were undecided or not ascertained on Q. 27 were regarded as undecided on the desired political status and were not tested for their attitude on Q. 48. The way Q. 48 is phrased, it seemed adequate to indicate the form of union envisaged by those who favored integration; it did not seem justifiable, however, to take Q. 48 as sole measure of whether integration was favored or not. Similarly, those who favored independent national policy were not tested further on Q. 48.

All respondents who could not be grouped clearly according to the two applied questions, like those for alliances but undecided about the form of the alliance, were also regarded as undecided on the desired political status.

To determine the attitude towards military integration, all respondents were tested on Q. 83, "What do you think of a conventionally equipped European army: Would you favor the EDC today?" The breakdown is evident from the chart. "Unconditional for military integration" comprises the responses "Favor generally (not excited about it)" and "Strongly favor (enthusiastic)." Since Q. 83 encompassed only one possible form of integration, European integration, Q. 57, "Should (Germany) (France) participate in such a NATO nuclear force, if such a force were created?" was used to determine those who were for integration within an Atlantic community. Respondents conditionally for military integration, according to Q. 83, were tested again on Q. 57 to ascertain whether they favored integration unconditionally where NATO was concerned.

Subtotal I was arrived at by determining whether any of the respondents, though favoring the preservation of national sovereignty, were for military integration. The applied questions were again Q. 83 and Q. 57; all favorable responses were counted as favoring integration. Subtotal II was obtained as indicated in the chart itself. Those who were neither nationalists nor for at least one form of integration

TABLE A:
Alternative Approaches to European Security: National Sovereignty, Arms Control and European or Atlantic Integration (A Simplified Tabulation)

A. *French Elite Responses (N = 147)*

Attitude toward European or Atlantic Arms Competition versus Control	European Orientation												Atlantic Orientation											
	Arms									Subtotal Europeans ④			Arms									Subtotal Atlantics ⑧		
	Competition ①			Control ②			DK ③						Competition ⑤			Control ⑥			DK ⑦					
	N	% of total	% of column	N	% of total	% of column	N	% of total	% of column	N	% of total	% of column	N	% of total	% of column	N	% of total	% of column	N	% of total	% of column	N	% of total	% of column
Sovereignty																								
1. Independent national policy	4	3	33	4	3	12	0	0	0	8	5	17	9	6	53	2	1	7	6	4	55	17	12	29
2. Alliances among sovereign nations	1	1	8	7	5	21	1	1	50	9	6	19	2	1	12	5	3	17	1	1	9	8	5	14
3. Integration (political) part of the way	1	1	8	1	1	3	0	0	0	2	1	4	1	1	6	8	5	27	1	1	9	10	7	17
4. Integration (political) all the way to federation	3	2	25	12	8	36	0	0	0	15	10	32	3	2	18	12	8	40	0	0	0	15	10	26
5. Undecided on desired political status	3	2	25	9	6	27	1	1	50	13	9	28	2	1	12	3	2	10	2	2	27	8	5	14
Military																								
6. For integration (military) conditional	3	2	25	10	7	30	1	1	50	14	10	30	3	2	18	6	4	20	5	3	45	14	10	24
7. Ditto: unconditional	1	1	8	1	1	3	0	0	0	2	1	4	2	1	12	9	6	30	3	2	27	14	10	24
8. Not for military integration or undecided	8	5	67	22	15	67	1	1	50	31	21	66	12	8	71	15	10	50	3	2	27	30	20	52
Subtotal 1: Preservers of sovereignty (1 + 2)	3	2	25	7	5	21	0	0	0	10	7	21	8	5	47	6	4	20	3	2	27	17	12	29
9. Complete																								
10. Partial (for military integration)	2	1	17	4	3	12	1	1	50	7	5	15	3	2	18	1	1	3	4	3	36	8	5	14
Subtotal 11: Integrationists																								
11. Partial (at least *a* for 3 or 6)	4	3	33	16	11	48	0	0	0	20	14	43	4	3	24	18	12	60	4	3	36	26	18	45
12. Complete (only 4 and 7)	0	0	0	0	0	0	0	0	0	0	0	0	1	1	6	4	3	13	0	0	0	5	3	9
Subtotal III:																								
13. Undecided on political and military status	3	2	25	6	4	18	1	1	50	10	7	21	1	1	6	1	1	3	0	0	0	2	1	3

Dependence on U.S.																								
14. Partial	1	1	8	2	1	6	0	0	0	3	2	6	6	4	35	3	2	10	5	3	45	14	10	24
15. Complete	11	7	92	28	19	85	2	1	100	41	28	87	9	6	53	18	12	60	6	4	55	33	22	57
16. No dependence seen or undecided	0	0	0	3	2	9	0	0	0	3	2	6	2	1	12	9	6	30	0	0	0	11	7	19
17. Grand totals: 1–5; 6–8; 9–12; 13–15; Subtotals I–III	12	8	100	33	22	100	2	1	100	47	32	100	17	12	100	30	20	100	11	7	100	58	39	100

A. *French Elite Responses* (*Continued*)

Attitude toward European or Atlantic Arms Competition versus Control	Pro-Europe and Pro-NATO												Neither			Total	
	Arms									⑫ Subtotal Pro-Europe and Pro-NATO							
	⑨ Competition			⑩ Control			⑪ DK						⑬			⑭	
Sovereignty	*N*	% of total	% of column	*N*	% of total	% of column	*N*	% of total	% of column	*N*	% of total	% of column	*N*	% of total	% of column	*N*	% of total
1. Independent national policy	0	0	0	5	3	29	1	1	17	6	4	22	6	4	40	37	25
2. Alliances among sovereign nations	0	0	0	1	1	6	1	1	17	2	1	7	4	3	27	23	16
3. Integration (political) part of the way	2	1	50	0	0	0	1	1	17	3	2	11	1	1	7	16	11
4. Ditto; All the way to federation	1	1	25	11	7	65	2	1	33	14	10	52	1	1	7	45	31
5. Undecided on desired political status	1	1	25	0	0	0	1	1	17	2	1	7	3	2	20	26	18
6. Integration (military) conditional	1	1	25	10	7	59	3	2	50	14	10	52	3	2	20	45	31
7. Ditto: Unconditional	2	1	50	4	3	24	2	1	33	8	5	30	0	0	0	24	16
8. Not for military integration or undecided	1	1	25	3	2	18	1	1	17	5	3	19	12	8	80	78	53
Subtotal I: Preservers of sovereignty (1 + 2)																	
9. Complete	0	0	0	2	1	12	0	0	0	2	1	7	9	6	60	38	26
10. Partial (for military integration)	0	0	0	4	3	24	2	1	33	6	4	22	1	1	7	22	15
Subtotal II: Integrationists																	
11. Partial (at least for 3 or 6)	4	3	100	7	5	41	3	2	50	14	10	52	3	2	20	63	43
12. Complete (only for 4 and 7)	0	0	0	4	3	24	1	1	17	5	3	19	0	0	0	10	7
13. Subtotal III: Undecided on political and military status	0	0	0	0	0	0	0	0	0	0	0	0	2	1	13	14	10
Dependence on U.S.																	
14. Partial	0	0	0	1	1	6	1	1	17	2	1	7	3	2	20	22	15
15. Complete	4	3	100	16	11	94	5	3	83	25	17	93	6	4	40	105	71
16. No dependence seen or undecided	0	0	0	0	0	0	0	0	0	0	0	0	6	4	40	20	14
17. Grand totals: 1–5; 6–8; 9–13; 14–16; Subtotals I–III	4	3	100	17	12	100	6	4	100	27	18	100	15	10	100	147	100

TABLE A (*Continued*)

B. *West German Elite Responses (N = 173)*

Attitude toward European or Atlantic Arms Competition versus Control	European Orientation												Atlantic Orientation											
	Arms									Subtotal Europeans ④			Arms									Subtotal Atlantics ⑧		
	Competition ①			Control ②			DK ③						Competition ⑤			Control ⑥			DK ⑦					
	N	% of total	% of column	N	% of total	% of column	N	% of total	% of column	N	% of total	% of column	N	% of total	% of column	N	% of total	% of column	N	% of total	% of column	N	% of total	% of column
Sovereignty																								
1. Independent national policy	3	2	38	3	2	13	0	0	0	6	3	19	0	0	0	1	1	2	0	0	0	1	1	1
2. Alliances among sovereign nations	1	1	13	3	2	13	0	0	0	4	2	13	3	2	18	11	6	20	0	0	0	14	8	19
3. Integration (political) Part of the way	2	1	25	0	0	0	0	0	0	2	1	6	3	2	18	18	10	32	0	0	0	21	12	28
4. Ditto. All the way to federation	2	1	25	12	7	52	0	0	0	14	8	45	11	6	65	23	13	41	1	1	100	35	20	47
5. Undecided on desired political status	0	0	0	5	3	22	0	0	0	5	3	16	0	0	0	3	2	5	0	0	0	3	2	4
6. For integration (military) conditional	1	1	13	3	2	13	0	0	0	4	2	13	3	2	18	6	3	11	0	0	0	9	5	12
7. Ditto: Unconditional	6	3	75	19	11	83	0	0	0	25	14	81	14	8	82	42	24	75	1	1	100	57	33	77
8. Not for military integration or undecided	1	1	13	1	1	4	0	0	0	2	1	6	0	0	0	8	5	14	0	0	0	8	5	11
Subtotal I: Preservers of sovereignty (1 + 2)	0	0	0	1	1	4	0	0	0	1	1	3	0	0	0	0	0	0	0	0	0	0	0	0
9. Complete	0	0	0	1	1	4	0	0	0	1	1	3	0	0	0	0	0	0	0	0	0	0	0	0
10. Partial (for military integration)	4	2	50	5	3	22	0	0	0	9	5	29	3	2	18	12	7	21	0	0	0	15	9	20
Sovereignty **Subtotal II: Integrationists**																								
11. Partial (at least for 3 or 6)	3	2	38	8	5	35	0	0	0	11	6	35	6	3	35	29	17	52	0	0	0	35	20	47
12. Complete (only for 4 and 7)	1	1	13	9	5	39	0	0	0	10	6	32	8	5	47	15	9	27	1	1	100	24	14	32
13. Subtotal III: Undecided on political and military status	0	0	0	0	0	0	0	0	0	0	0	0	0	0	0	0	0	0	0	0	0	0	0	0

Dependence on U.S. (continued)

	Competition (9) N	% of total	% of column	Control (10) N	% of total	% of column	DK (11) N	% of total	% of column	Subtotal Pro-Europe and Pro-NATO (12) N	% of total	% of column	Neither (13) N	% of total	% of column	Total (14) N	% of total
14. Partial	0	0	0	0	0	0	2	1	8	2	1	4	0	0	0	2	3
15. Complete	8	5	100	21	12	91	23	13	92	52	30	93	17	10	94	69	93
16. No dependence seen or undecided	0	0	0	2	1	9	0	0	0	2	1	4	1	1	6	3	4
17. Grand totals: 1–5; 6–8; 9–13; 14–16; Subtotals I–III	8	5	100	23	13	100	25	14	100	56	32	100	18	10	100	74	100

B. West German Elite Responses (Continued)

Attitude toward European or Atlantic Arms Competition versus Control

Sovereignty	Pro-Europe and Pro-NATO — Arms — Competition (9) N	% of total	% of column	Control (10) N	% of total	% of column	DK (11) N	% of total	% of column	Subtotal Pro-Europe and Pro-NATO (12) N	% of total	% of column	Neither (13) N	% of total	% of column	Total (14) N	% of total
1. Independent national policy	1	1	13	1	1	3	0	0	0	2	1	4	2	1	11	11	6
2. Alliances among sovereign nations	0	0	0	5	5	23	0	0	0	9	5	18	2	1	11	29	17
3. Integration (political) part of the way	1	1	13	5	5	23	0	0	0	10	6	20	5	3	26	38	22
4. Ditto: All the way to federation	4	2	50	11	11	48	1	1	100	24	14	49	5	3	26	78	45
5. Undecided on desired political status	2	1	25	1	1	5	0	0	0	4	2	8	5	3	26	17	10
6. Integration (military) conditional	1	1	13	2	2	8	0	0	0	4	2	8	3	2	16	20	12
7. Ditto: Unconditional	6	3	75	14	14	60	0	0	0	30	17	61	3	2	16	115	66
8. No for military integration or undecided	1	1	13	8	8	33	1	1	100	15	9	31	13	8	68	38	22
Subtotal I: Preservers of Sovereignty (1 + 2)																	
9. Complete	0	0	0	1	1	5	0	0	0	2	1	4	2	2	21	7	4
10. Partial (for military integration)	1	1	13	5	5	20	0	0	0	9	5	18	0	0	0	33	19
Subtotal II: Integrationists																	
11. Partial (at least for 3 or 6)	3	2	38	10	10	43	1	1	100	21	12	43	10	6	53	77	45
12. Complete (only for 4 and 7)	4	2	50	7	7	30	0	0	0	16	9	33	1	1	5	51	29
13. Subtotal III: Undecided on political and military status	0	0	0	1	1	3	0	0	0	1	1	2	4	2	21	5	3
Dependence on U.S.																	
14. Partial	0	0	0	0	0	0	0	0	0	0	0	0	0	0	0	2	1
15. Complete	8	5	100	21	21	90	1	1	100	45	26	92	13	8	68	156	90
16. No dependence seen or undecided	0	0	0	2	2	10	0	0	0	4	2	8	6	3	32	15	9
17. Grand totals: 1–5; 6–8; 9–13; 14–16; Subtotals I–III	8	5	100	23	23	100	1	1	100	49	28	100	19	11	100	173	100

are shown under Subtotal III: "Undecided on political and military status."

To enable the reader to compare the distributions for national action and integration with the feelings of dependence on the U.S., a seventh item was included, which shows a breakdown according to Q. 75, "To what extent would (Germany's) (France's) military security ultimately depend upon the American deterrent?" Respondents were listed as feeling partially dependent on the American deterrent if they answered "Ultimately depends upon American deterrent only to a limited extent." Respondents who answered "Ultimately depends completely" and "In large measure upon American deterrent" form the group "Complete dependence."

Appendix B

Most European leaders cannot be interviewed effectively by the mechanical application of a rigid questionnaire. They prefer to express their thoughts in their own way, in conversation with questioners whom they can accept as serious and reasonably well informed. Accordingly, all our interviewers were American academic specialists who had spent years of work studying the country whose elite members they were not interviewing. The interviews were free in form but rather carefully guided in substance. They were based on the list of questions that follows. This list of questions was both in the mind and in the pocket of the interviewer but it was not shown to the respondent, so as not to destroy his spontaneity. Rather, each major topic or group question was opened by the interviewer who then let the respondent proceed on his own. When any topics on the questionnaire were not covered spontaneously by the respondent, the interviewer usually would ask a question directed to the topic, and if not successful, he might try a second time. Immediately after each interview—which lasted on the average about one-and-one-half hours—the interviewer would dictate a summary of the interview on his tape recorder, and he would fill out all the questions on his questionnaire for the interview of this particular respondent. In doing so, the interviewer would also state specifically on which questions the respondent had been undecided, uninformed, or evasive, and further, on which questions his views had not been ascertained, either because the respondent had avoided talking about them, or because the interview had gone in a different direction. The numbers of such cases for each question are reported in Appendix C.

The questions thus were not all "asked" formally, but the interviewers recorded in their notes immediately after each interview whether and how they thought that the respondents, speaking freely in their own words, had answered them. This method of combining freedom of expression for the respondent with comprehensiveness of coverage and comparability for coding purposes represents the best practicable compromise that we could find in terms of modern survey research practice. It depended heavily on the alertness, insight, reliability and good judgment of our eight interviewers. (Cross-checks, comparing the distributions of responses obtained by each of them with those elicited by the others did not suggest any significant deviations or irregularities.)[1]

With these cautions, our list of questions is reproduced on the following pages. Together with the answers recorded by the interviewers, it represents the best evidence that could be obtained within our limits of time and resources concerning views of French and German leaders in mid-1964.

The views of the respondents usually were first tabulated in a nine-step code, distinguishing: 1. enthusiastic support, 2. definite support, 3. conditional support, 4. undecided or "don't know" responses, 5. conditional opposition, 6. definite opposition, 7. vehement opposition, 8. "don't know," and 9. "not ascertained." For certain analytic purposes, these tabulations were summarized in a five-step scheme: 1. definite support $(1 + 2)$, conditional support (3), 3. undecided or uninformed $(4, 8)$, 4. conditional opposition (5), 5. definite opposition $(6, 7)$. If the proportion of respondents whose views had not been ascertained was no more than 5% of the total, it was added to the undecided or uninformed. Otherwise, the number was reported separately and the percentages of responses were calculated only for the "articulate" respondents on this particular question, i.e., of those whose views on this point had been ascertained.

Such summary tables were prepared for a selection of the most interesting questions, marked with an asterisk in the list of questions that follows. These summary tables are then given in Appendix C.

More detailed tabulations of all coded responses are available in Karl W. Deutsch, Lewis J. Edinger, Roy C. Macridis, Richard L. Merritt and Helga Voss-Eckermann, *French and German Elite Responses, 1964: Codebook and Data,* (Yale University, Political Science Research Library, 1966, multigraphed, available on microfilm.) The version given here in this appendix includes a few very minor corrections of some of the tables given there such as Questions 39, 58, 71 and 80.

---

[1] Further details of our methods are reported in K. W. Deutsch, L. J. Edinger, R. C. Macridis, and R. L. Merritt, *France, Germany and the Western Alliance,* New York, Charles Scribner's Sons, 1967, Chapter 1.

QUESTION   (* indicates summary table of responses given in Appendix C)

* 1.   Are you content with the present governmental system in (the Federal Republic of Germany) (France)?

  2.   What are the positive features of the present form of government?

  3.   What are the negative features of the present governmental system? (Not asked explicitly in France.)

* 4.   What are the most important cleavages and conflicts in (German) (French) politics today?

* 5.   Is the conflict between left and right important today? (Asked in France only.)

* 6.   Which group or groups do you feel have gained in political power over the last few years?

* 7.   To what extent is the governmental system changing due to the changing influence of groups?

* 8.   Are the old parties dead? (Asked in France only.)

* 9.   Do you expect a revival of the Popular Front? (Asked in France only.)

*10.   Would you favor a revival of the Popular Front? (Asked in France only.)

*11.   Is Nazism dead? (Asked in Germany only.)

*12.   Is a revival of Nazism possible? (Asked in Germany only.)

 13.   What are the most important differences between the major political parties?

14.   What would be likely developments in French
            domestic politics over the next ten years? Will
            the Fifth Republic survive after de Gaulle?
            (Asked in France only.)

*15.   What will the role of the parties be after de
            Gaulle? (Asked in France only.)

16.   What would be likely developments in German
            domestic politics over the next ten years? Will
            either the Federal Government or the Länder
            gain more strength, or will there be no change?
            (Asked in Germany only.)

17.   Will the Chancellor (Executive) increasingly
            dominate the Bundestag (Legislature) during the
            next ten years, or vice versa, or will there be
            no change? (Germany)

*18.   Will the cohesiveness of the CDU increase or
            decrease in the next few years, or will it remain
            about the same? (Asked in Germany only.)

*19.   What are the prospects for an SPD government
            in the next ten years? (Asked in Germany only.)

20.   Would an SPD government bring about a differ-
            ence in the German political system? [In some
            cases, "important" differences in German
            "policy."] (Asked in Germany only.)

21.   How will (German) (French) society react to a
            major upheaval in the world? Type of upheaval
            inferred by respondent? (In Germany, in ab-
            sence of inference, it was asked for specif-
            ically.)

22.   Society's reaction to the upheaval?

23.   Which basic strengths of the society are likely
            to come to the surface in time of crisis?

24.   Which basic weaknesses of the society are likely
            to come to the surface in time of crisis?

*25.   Some people say that the domination of world politics by America and Russia is disappearing. They say that in the future, as in the past, many nations will again be masters of their own independent foreign policies. How do you perceive the structures of the world political arena?

*26.   Do you welcome the current trend in world politics?

*27.   Do you feel that for a nation like (Germany) (France) an independent foreign policy is outmoded, or does every nation have to act by its national interest alone, even at the expense of international cooperation?

*28.   What is the best way to defend (German) (French) national interests at the present time?

*29.   Will the policies suggested for defending national interest continue to be feasible in the future?

*30.   What are the most important features of German foreign policy (in terms of government goals)? (Asked in Germany only.)

*31.   Are you satisfied with the government's foreign policy measures?

*32.   What developments in domestic policy are likely to bring about a change in (German) (French) foreign policy?

*33.   Which features of (German) (French) foreign policy, if any, are likely to remain after (Erhard) (de Gaulle)?

*34.   Does France have a "manifest destiny"? (Asked in France only.)

*35.   With which of the following countries will (Germany) (France) continue to share common interests for a long period?

*36.   What are the major sources of possible friction between the United States and (Germany) (France)?

*37.   Many people consider the reunification of Ger-
            many one of the world's most critical unsolved
            international problems. How do you feel about
            the whole question of German reunification?

*38.   What do you perceive French interest to be in
            the reunification of Germany? (Asked in France
            only.)

*39.   Do you expect German reunification within the
            next 25 years?

40.   Do you think that the status of Berlin will be
            changed in the next few years? If so, how?

41.   Expected form of change in status of Berlin? (If
            some change was expected in reply to question
            40.)

*42.   Would the recognition of East Germany ease
            international tension?

*43.   How would recognition of the Oder-Neisse Line
            affect efforts toward German reunification?

*44.   Would recognition of the Oder-Neisse Line ease
            tension in Central Europe?

*45.   Do you expect an appreciable change in relations
            between (Germany) (France) and the countries of
            Eastern Europe during the next years?

*46.   Most people agree that since World War II the
            general trend in Western Europe has been to-
            ward limiting national sovereignties in favor of
            international associations. To what extent is
            (German) (French) politics oriented in this
            direction?

*47.   To what extent do you consider efforts in this
            direction to be sensible?

*48.   There is much discussion nowadays about
            European integration. Suggestions have been
            made concerning different forms of European
            unity (cooperation) ranging all the way from
            simple cooperation among sovereign states to
            the merging of all states into one centralized
            European state. What form of union most nearly
            describes an integrated Europe as you generally
            think of it?

*49.   In your opinion, which countries should be in-
        cluded in such a European union?

*50.   Is European integration likely to be achieved
        within the next ten years?

51.   What will the map of Europe look like in 1975?
        (Asked in France only.)

*52.   What, in your thinking, would be the primary
        value of a united Europe? That is, what do you
        think is the purpose of European integration?

*53.   At the present time to what extent can (Germany)
        (France) rely upon NATO to protect her?

*54.   Could NATO be reformed in such a way that
        (Germany) (France) can rely on it for protection?
        How?

*55.   Do you feel that (Germany) (France) should
        rather endeavor to strengthen NATO, or Euro-
        pean unity (EEC), or both?

*56.   What do you think of the widely-discussed pro-
        posal of a multilateral nuclear force under
        NATO command?

*57.   Should (Germany) (France) participate in such a
        NATO nuclear force, if such a force were
        created?

*58.   French version: Who should control the nuclear
        force for NATO?

        German version: Should all members of the
        Alliance have the same say about where and
        when NATO nuclear weapons are used and under
        whose command should such a NATO nuclear
        force be?

*59.   German version: To what extent can Germany
        rely upon France as an ally?

        French version: To what extent can France rely
        upon Germany as an ally?

60.   How would the demise of de Gaulle affect German
        confidence in France as an ally? (Asked in
        Germany only.)

61.   How would the demise of de Gaulle affect French confidence in Germany as an ally? (Asked in France only.)

*62.   What is the greatest threat to (German) (French) security at the present time?

*63.   What kind of a threat is this?

64.   For how long do you think this threat will continue?

*65.   In what form is there a military threat?

*66.   In your opinion, what would be the best defense against this threat?

*67.   It is often said that a national deterrent is a prerequisite of a country's independence. Do you share this view?

*68.   Is an independent deterrent a condition for German national independence? (Asked in France only.)

*69.   Is a national deterrent a condition of French independence in particular? (Asked in Germany only.)

*70.   Is an independent deterrent necessary for a nation's prestige in the world? (In Germany: In what sense would a national deterrent affect the Federal Republic's prestige in the world?)

*71.   Is an independent deterrent worth the cost?

*72.   Is (Would) a national deterrent (be) credible to (Germany's) (France's) enemies?

*73.   What would happen to the force de frappe if de Gaulle left the political scene? (Asked in France only.)

*74.   If de Gaulle and his force de frappe should disappear, what would be the effect on Germany? (Asked in Germany only.)

*75.   To what extent would (Germany's) (France's) military security ultimately depend upon the American deterrent? (In many of the German interviews, the phrase "even in the presence of a national deterrent" was added.)

*76.   In which circumstances do you think America will use her deterrent?

77.   What do you think of an isolationist "Fortress America" policy of the United States?

*78.   Do you think it is likely that the United States will some day abandon its commitments for the defense of Western Europe?

*79.   Do you think that efforts should be made to halt the proliferation of nuclear weapons to countries that do not now possess them?

*80.   In your view, which countries should possess nuclear weapons?

81.   What would be your reaction in the event that East Germany or another East European country should acquire nuclear weapons? (Asked in Germany only.)

*82.   Would you favor a European nuclear force independent of NATO?

*83.   What do you think of a conventionally equipped European army? Would you favor the EDC today?

*84.   The U.S.A. and Russia recently concluded a bilateral agreement banning nuclear testing in the atmosphere. Do you approve or disapprove of this East-West agreement?

*85.   How do you feel about (Germany) (France) not being consulted?

*86.   Would you favor further arms control agreements between the U.S. and the U.S.S.R.?

87.   Should (Germany) (France) be consulted in negotiations for further arms control agreements of this kind?

*88.   Would you favor further arms control agree-
        ments even if your country is not consulted?

*89.   For years both East and West have been offering
        alternative schemes for arms control and dis-
        armament, some of them dealing with problems
        of arms control in Europe and others more
        universal in scope. Of which of these have you
        heard most?

*90.   Which of the various arms control and disarm-
        ament plans would you favor?

*91.   Would the de-nuclearization of Central Europe
        ease the threat of military conflict there?

*92.   What do you think about the complete neutraliza-
        tion of Central Europe?

*93.   Should foreign troops be withdrawn from both
        Eastern and Western Europe?

*94.   Should an East-West agreement on arms control
        be coupled with inspection?

 95.   In your opinion, what kind of inspection would be
        most feasible?

 96.   Is it possible that arms control agreements
        would somehow endanger the security of Berlin?

 97.   Would you favor such agreements even if they
        endangered the security of Berlin?

*98.   Do you think it is possible to ease international
        tension by disarmament, or is the whole ques-
        tion of disarmament and arms control a mere
        utopia not worth discussing?

Appendix C

Germany		France		Code
N	%	N	%	
				Q. 1. Are you content with the pre-sent governmental system in (the Federal Republic of Germany) (France)?
128	74	40	27	A. Satisfied
33	19	38	26	B. Moderately satisfied (good in general, but some changes would be desirable)
5	3	11	8	C. Indifferent, DK**, N.A.†
7	4	25	17	D. Moderately dissatisfied (idea good, but many bad features)
0	0	33	22	E. Dissatisfied
173	100%	147	100%	

**Don't know.

† Not ascertained.

Germany		France		Code
N	%	N	%	

Q. 4. What are the most important cleavages and conflicts in (German) (French) politics today? (Three possible responses.)

Germany		France		Code
21	6	74	22	A. Class, ideological
59	17	81	24	B. Fundamental domestic political issue, constitutional amendments
117	34	70	21	C. Current domestic political issue, party political, social welfare policy
25	7	42	12	D. European integration problems
54	16	2	1	E. Atlantic community problems
11	3	4	1	F. Armament issues
37	11	8	2	G. Policy toward East, Communism
23	7	39	12	H. DK (first response), none (first response), cleavage between generations, other cleavages, other foreign policy cleavages, opponents of decolonization, modernization versus immobility, agriculture; peasant disaffection, religion; secularism, reason versus authoritarianism, institutions, finances
0	0	17	5	K. Characteristics/Personality of de Gaulle
347	101%	337	100%	
2		8		Not ascertained (on first response)
58		33		No second type of cleavage given
112		63		No third type of cleavage given
519		441		

Germany N	%	France N	%	Code
				Q. 5. Is the conflict between left and right important today? (Asked in France only.)
		71	51	A. Yes
		1	1	B. DK or undecided
		68	49	C. No
		140	101%	
		7		Not ascertained
		147		
				Q. 6. Which group or groups do you feel have gained in political power over the last few years?
10	4	17	7	A. Right wing elements, Army, Gaullists, UNR
0	0	1	0	B. Left wing elements, Communists
14	6	111	43	C. Bureaucracy, technocracy
29	12	70	27	D. Business interests financial and industrial, international cartels
28	12	3	1	E. Parties, interest groups in general
33	14	17	7	F. Trade unions; labor interests, less privileged
0	0	15	6	G. Youth, women
28	12	14	5	H. Farmers, middle class
95	40	11	4	K. Miscellaneous
237	100%	259	100%	
14		17		Not ascertained (on first response)
118		60		No second group given
150		105		No third group given
519		441		

Germany		France		Code
N	%	N	%	

Q. 7. To what extent is the governmental system changing due to the changing influence of groups?

Germany		France		
2	1	15	12	A. Fundamental (systemic/structural) change
46	32	26	20	B. Noticeable change (functional; won't change system)
91	64	84	66	C. Some (minor) change (functional), no change at all
3	2	2	2	D. DK
142	99%	127	100%	
31		20		Not ascertained
173		147		

Q. 8. Are the old parties dead? (Asked in France only.)

		France		
		35	24	A. Yes
		103	70	B. No
		9	6	C. DK, undecided
		147	100%	

Q. 9. Do you expect a revival of the Popular Front? (Asked in France only.)

		France		
		39	35	A. Yes
		10	9	B. DK or undecided
		64	57	C. No
		113	101%	
		34		Not ascertained
		147		

Germany		France		
N	%	N	%	Code
				Q. 10. Would you favor a revival of the Popular Front? (Asked in France only.)
		26	18	A. Favor
		30	21	B. Indifferent (undecided), DK
		85	60	C. Oppose
		141	99%	
		6		Not ascertained
		147		
				Q. 11. Is Nazism dead? (Asked in Germany only.)
132	87			A. Yes
6	4			B. Yes, conditionally
1	1			C. Undecided, DK
13	9			D. No
152	101%			
21				Not ascertained
173				
				Q. 12. Is a revival of Nazism possible? (Asked in Germany only.)
0	0			A. Strong possibility
37	24			B. Moderate possibility
43	28			C. Possible as radical nationalism or in modified form
74	48			D. No possibility at all
0	0			E. DK
154	100%			
19				Not ascertained
173				

| Germany | | France | | Code |
N	%	N	%	
				Q. 15. What will the role of the parties be after de Gaulle? (Asked in France only.)
		72	46	A. More important than at present
		52	33	B. No change or undecided
		32	21	C. Less important
		156	100%	
		8		Not ascertained (on first response)
		130		No second response given
		294		
				Q. 18. Will the cohesiveness of the CDU increase or decrease in the next few years, or will it remain about the same? (Asked in Germany only.)
75	49			A. As cohesive as at present or become more so
57	37			B. Will become less cohesive than at present
22	14			C. DK
154	100%			
19				Not ascertained
173				

Germany		France		
N	%	N	%	Code
				Q. 19. What are the prospects for an SPD government in the next ten years? (Asked in Germany only.)
63	40			A. Likely
39	25			B. Depends (unlikely under certain specific conditions; likely only under certain specific conditions), DK
57	36			C. Unlikely
159	101%			
14				Not ascertained
173				
				Q. 25. Some people say that the domination of world politics by America and Russia is disappearing. They say that in the future, as in the past, many nations will again be masters of their own independent foreign policies. How do you perceive the structures of the world political arena?
114	66	34	23	A. Bipolarity will remain or increase
52	30	108	73	B. Becoming increasingly multipolar (moving toward a new balance of power)
7	4	5	3	C. DK, N.A.
173	100%	147	99%	

Germany		France		Code
N	%	N	%	

				Q. 26. Do you welcome the current trend in world politics?
93	54	89	61	A. Favors current trend
24	14	30	20	B. Favors current trend, but with considerable reservation
29	17	11	7	C. Doesn't care, undecided, DK, N.A.
5	3	10	7	D. Against current trend conditionally
22	13	7	5	E. Against current trend
173	101%	147	100%	

				Q. 27. Do you feel that for a nation like (Germany) (France) an independent foreign policy is outmoded, or does every nation have to act by its national interest alone, even at the expense of international cooperation?
6	3	17	12	A. Favors independent national action
5	3	20	14	B. Favors national action conditionally (if certain conditions prevail or develop)
9	5	20	14	C. Indifferent, undecided, DK, N.A.
16	9	26	18	D. Favors cooperation in alliances conditionally (if certain conditions prevail or develop)
137	79	64	44	E. Favors cooperation in alliances
173	99%	147	102%	

Germany		France		Code
N	%	N	%	

Q. 28. What is the best way to defend (German) (French) national interests at the present time? (Cumulation of three possible responses.)

Germany		France		Code
0	0	59	19	A. National defense (atomic)
11	7	36	11	B. National defense (conventional), diplomacy, withdrawal from international affairs (isolation)
154	92	212	67	C. International diplomacy (UN, EEC, etc.), defense (alliance), defense (integrated forces, e.g., EDC)
3	2	10	3	D. International arms control
0	0	0	0	E. DK
168	101%	317	100%	
5		1		Not ascertained (on first response)
173		30		No second response on defense given
173		93		No third response on defense given
519		441		

Q. 29. Will the policies suggested for defending national interest continue to be feasible in the future?

Germany		France		Code
154	96	102	72	A. Yes
4	2	23	16	B. Yes, under certain conditions
2	1	15	11	C. Undecided, DK
1	1	2	1	D. No
161	100%	142	100%	
12		5		Not ascertained
173		147		

| Germany | | France | | Code |
N	%	N	%	
				Q. 30. What are the most important features of German foreign policy (in terms of government goals)? (Asked in Germany only.)
123	31			A. German sovereignty, diplomacy, economic and commercial policies, security, reunification
114	29			B. German-American relations, cooperation with the West
35	9			C. Franco-German relations
3	1			D. Anglo-German relations
69	17			E. European integration
43	11			F. German-Soviet relations, relations with Eastern Europe
8	2			G. Relations with underdeveloped countries, reparations to Israel, other, DK
395	100%			
16				Not ascertained
34				No second feature given
74				No third feature given
519				
				Q. 31. Are you satisfied with the government's foreign policy measures?
95	55	49	33	A. Approval of regime's foreign policy
33	19	25	17	B. Mild approval (more good features than bad)
11	6	5	3	C. Indifference, undecided, doesn't care, DK, N.A.
10	6	16	11	D. Mild disapproval
24	14	52	35	E. Disapproval
173	100%	147	99%	

| Germany | | France | | Code |
N	%	N	%	
				Q. 32. What developments in domestic policy are likely to bring about a change in (German) (French) foreign policy?
13	8	176	54	A. National leader (Erhard) (de Gaulle) or government leaves political scene
14	8	18	6	B. Ascendancy of right wing factions
7	4	46	14	C. Ascendancy of left wing factions
65	38	2	1	D. Ascendancy of some specific group or person
1	1	57	17	E. Increased supranational commitment
2	1	3	1	F. Decreased supranational commitment
5	3	22	7	G. Economic trends
53	31	1	0	H. None (on first response)
11	6	1	0	K. Miscellaneous
171	100%	326	100%	
49		8		Not ascertained (on first response)
138		34		No second development given
161		73		No third development given
519		441		

Germany		France		Code
N	%	N	%	

<table>
<tr><td colspan="5">Q. 33. Which features of (German) (French) foreign policy, if any, are likely to remain after (Erhard) (de Gaulle)?</td></tr>
</table>

Germany N	Germany %	France N	France %	Code
54	30	104	34	A. Policy toward United States and NATO
9	5	46	15	B. Policy toward East
31	17	82	27	C. Franco-German rapprochement and policy toward European integration
1	1	37	12	D. Policy toward non-Western countries
55	31	6	2	E. All features (on first response)
22	12	19	6	F. Other (on second and third responses) and DK (on first response)
6	3	15	5	G. No features (on first response)
178	99%	309	101%	
47		4		Not ascertained (on first response)
0		9		No first feature given
139		47		No second feature given
155		72		No third feature given
519		441		

<table>
<tr><td colspan="5">Q. 34. Does France have a "Manifest Destiny"? (Asked in France only.)</td></tr>
</table>

Germany N	Germany %	France N	France %	Code
		59	53	A. Yes
		1	1	B. DK
		52	46	C. No
		112	100%	
		35		Not ascertained
		147		

Germany		France		
N	%	N	%	Code

Q. 35. With which of the following countries will (Germany) (France) continue to share common interests for a long period?

Germany		France		
99	24	77	19	A. Western and Northern European countries except Russia, EFTA countries
49	12	55	14	B. (In Germany: France) (In France: Germany)
150	36	129	32	C. United States, Free World, NATO countries
29	7	11	3	D. Poland, Socialist countries, Russia, Eastern Europe, all European including Russia
69	17	130	32	E. EEC countries, neighbor countries
7	2	4	1	F. Developing countries, South America, French speaking countries of the "Third World"
10	2	0	0	G. Other, no other country, DK
413	100%	406	101%	
6		2		Not ascertained (on first response)
24		4		No second country given
76		29		No third country given
519		441		

| Germany | | France | | Code |
N	%	N	%	
				Q. 36. What are the major sources of possible friction between the United States and (Germany) (France)?
5	2	96	29	A. Desire for independent nuclear force
42	16	108	32	B. NATO policy, policies concerning European unity, policy toward France (in Germany only)
14	5	60	18	C. Policy toward non-Western countries (excluding China), policy toward China, worldwide policy commitments of U.S.A., Southeast Asia
115	43	3	1	D. Reunification and Eastern territories; Berlin question, withdrawal of U.S. troops, policy toward Russia, cost of U.S. troops in Germany and development aid, policy toward Eastern Europe
51	19	20	6	E. Trade policies
24	9	4	1	F. No recognizable friction (first response)
0	0	19	6	G. Personal characteristics of de Gaulle
8	3	23	7	H. French desire for greater independence
10	4	3	1	K. DK (on first response), other
269	101%	336	101%	
11		3		Not ascertained (on first response)
97		33		No second source of friction
142		69		No third source of friction
519		441		

Germany		France		Code
N	%	N	%	

Q. 37. Many people consider the reunification of Germany as one of the world's most critical unsolved international problems. How do you feel about the whole question of German reunification?

Germany		France		
132	77	8	7	A. Favor
22	13	35	32	B. Conditionally in favor (if certain conditions prevail or develop)
5	3	7	6	C. Indifferent, undecided, DK, evasive
10	6	29	27	D. Conditionally against (other things take precedence, such as freedom for East Germany; also, in Germany, "Jaspers' argument") *
2	1	30	28	E. Against
171	100%	109	100%	
2		38		Not ascertained
173		147		

*On the grounds that reunification may be far away, the German philosopher Karl Jaspers has proposed as a more urgent practical goal the early liberalization of the East German regime through increased West German contacts.

Q. 38. What do you perceive French interest to be in the reunification of Germany? (Asked in France only.)

		France		
		45	58	A. Reunified Germany would be a threat to French security
		25	32	B. Reunification would enhance French security
		7	9	C. DK
		77	99%	
		70		Not ascertained
		147		

Germany		France		Code
N	%	N	%	

Q. 39. Do you expect German re-unification within the next 25 years?

Germany		France		Code
32	20	2	2	A. Germany will regain her unity within the next 25 years
63	38	10	11	B. Germany will regain her unity within the next 25 years if certain conditions prevail or develop
47	29	76	83	C. Germany will not regain her unity within the next 25 years, probably never
22	13	4	4	D. DK
164	100%	92	100%	
9		55		Not ascertained
173		147		

Q. 42. Would the recognition of East Germany ease international tension?

Germany		France		Code
38	25	10	18	A. Would ease tensions
52	34	27	49	B. Would not affect tensions
41	27	14	25	C. Likely to increase international tensions or lead to war
22	14	4	7	D. DK, evasive
153	100%	55	99%	
20		92		Not ascertained
173		147		

Germany		France		Code
N	%	N	%	

Q. 43. How would recognition of the Oder-Neisse Line affect efforts toward German reunification?

Germany		France		Code
63	41	8	16	A. Would help
57	37	30	60	B. Would make no difference
16	10	7	14	C. Would hinder
17	11	5	10	D. DK, evasive
153	99%	50	100%	
20		97		Not ascertained
173		147		

Q. 44. Would the recognition of the Oder-Neisse Line affect tension in Central Europe?

Germany		France		Code
80	52	22	42	A. Yes
52	34	15	29	B. Not at all
13	8	6	12	C. Likely to increase tensions
10	6	9	17	D. DK, evasive
155	100%	52	100%	
18		95		Not ascertained
173		147		

Germany		France		
N	%	N	%	Code
				Q. 45. Do you expect an appreciable change in relations between (Germany) (France) and the countries of Eastern Europe during the next years?
134	83	117	99	A. More cordial
28	17	0	0	B. No change expected, DK
0	0	1	1	C. Less cordial
162	100%	118	100%	
11		29		Not ascertained
173		147		
				Q. 46. Most people agree that since World War II the general trend in Western Europe has been toward limiting national sovereignties in favor of international associations. To what extent is (German) (French) politics oriented in this direction?
96	55	2	1	A. National policies decidedly oriented toward further limitations of sovereignty
71	41	16	11	B. Some policies oriented toward supranationalism; others not, DK, N.A.
6	3	129	88	C. Policies increasingly nationalistic in flavor
173	99%	147	100%	

| Germany | | France | | Code |
N	%	N	%	
				Q. 47. To what extent do you consider efforts in this direction to be sensible?
122	71	66	45	A. In favor of further limitations of sovereignty
34	20	56	38	B. Conditionally in favor of sovereignty (not excited about it)
9	5	4	3	C. Indifferent, undecided, N.A.
4	2	8	5	D. Conditionally against further limitations of sovereignty
4	2	13	9	E. Opposed
173	100%	147	100%	
				Q. 48. What form of union most nearly describes an integrated Europe as you think of it?
36	21	69	41	A. Loose international system with national dominance
42	25	26	15	B. Confederation
87	51	72	43	C. Supranational dominance, federal system, unitary European state
5	3	2	1	D. DK
170	100%	169	100%	
3		8		Not ascertained (on first response)
173		117		No second form of union given
346		294		

Germany		France		Code
N	%	N	%	

Q. 49. In your opinion, which countries should be included in such a European union?

23	13	33	22	A.	France and Germany, the Six, Western Europe except England
96	55	91	62	B.	The Six, plus England and other European countries
20	12	0	0	C.	Europe of the Council of Europe, Spain
23	13	11	7	D.	Europe including Eastern European countries
11	6	12	8	E.	Other, DK, N.A.
173	99%	147	99%		

Q. 50. Is European integration likely to be achieved within the next ten years?

73	46	27	19	A.	Will be achieved
30	19	44	31	B.	Depends (e.g., on de Gaulle's successor), DK
55	35	70	49	C.	Will not be achieved
158	100%	141	99%		
15		6			Not ascertained
173		147			

Germany		France		Code
N	%	N	%	
				Q. 52. What do you think is the purpose of European integration?
112	67	162	45	A. Economic betterment, more strength to solve European problems, unity of "Occident"
37	22	124	35	B. To strengthen European political power
17	10	67	19	C. To strengthen West against Communism
2	1	4	1	D. No purpose, DK
168	100%	357	100%	
5		3		Not ascertained (on first response)
173		26		No second purpose given
173		55		No third purpose given
519		441		
				Q. 53. At the present time to what extent can (Germany) (France) rely upon NATO to protect her?
112	65	92	63	A. Can rely upon NATO
52	30	48	33	B. Can be relied upon only under certain conditions, DK, N.A.
9	5	7	5	C. Cannot be relied upon
173	100%	147	101%	

Germany		France		Code
N	%	N	%	

Q. 54. Could NATO be reformed in such a way that (Germany) (France) can rely on it for protection? How?

Germany		France		
53	38	3	3	A. Needs no reform
37	26	38	32	B. NATO should be strengthened, become better integrated, more equality
8	6	3	3	C. Germany alone or together with other countries should have more influence
11	8	20	17	D. Hopeless, outmoded
15	11	7	6	E. Other reform, DK
3	2	31	26	F. Countries other than Germany should have more influence
13	9	15	13	G. European or all members should have more influence
140	100%	117	100%	
33		30		Not ascertained
173		147		

Q. 55. Do you feel that (Germany) (France) should rather endeavor to strengthen NATO, or European unity (EEC), or both?

Germany		France		
15	11	5	4	A. Work primarily to strengthen NATO
102	72	61	49	B. Work to strengthen both
20	15	50	40	C. Work primarily to strengthen European unity (EEC)
4	3	8	7	D. Negative answers
141	101%	124	100%	
32		23		Not ascertained
173		147		

Germany		France		Code
N	%	N	%	
				Q. 56. What do you think of the widely discussed proposal of a multilateral nuclear force under NATO command?
58	34	18	18	A. Favor
22	13	21	21	B. Favor conditionally
28	16	24	24	C. Indifferent; undecided, DK
5	3	10	10	D. Opposed conditionally
58	34	27	27	E. Opposed
171	100%	100	100%	
2		47		Not ascertained
173		147		
				Q. 57. Should (Germany) (France) participate in such a NATO nuclear force, if such a force were created?
93	58	16	16	A. Definitely yes
20	13	44	43	B. Conditionally yes
12	8	12	12	C. Undecided, DK
8	5	21	21	D. Conditionally no
27	17	9	9	E. Definitely no
160	101%	102	101%	
13		45		Not ascertained
173		147		

Germany N	%	France N	%	Code
				Q. 58. French version: Who should control the nuclear force for NATO?
		12	16	A. United States alone
		0	0	B. With Britain
		41	55	C. United States, Great Britain, and France
		15	20	D. United States with Britain and Germany; United States, Britain, France, and Germany; all nations of the Alliance; or special NATO body.
		6	8	E. DK
		74	99%	
		73		Not ascertained
		147		
				Q. 58. German version: Should all members of the Alliance have the same say about where and when NATO nuclear weapons are used and under whose command should such a NATO nuclear force be?
				A. Control (command) of NATO nuclear force
84	56			A. United States
3	2			B. United States and Britain
1	1			C. United States, Great Britain, and France
56	37			D. United States with Britain and Germany; United States, Britain, France, and Germany; Britain, France, Germany, and Italy
6	4			E. DK
150	100%			
23				Not ascertained
173				

| Germany | | France | | Code |
N	%	N	%	
				Q. 59. German version: To what extent can Germany rely on France as an ally?
				French version: To what extent can France rely on Germany as an ally?
44	29	11	9	A. A great deal
50	33	115	85	B. To a limited extent
59	39	10	7	C. Not at all
153	100%	136	100%	
20		11		Not ascertained
173		147		
				Q. 62. What is the greatest threat to (German) (French) security at the present time?
1	1	8	5	A. United States
121	70	111	76	B. Communist country
2	1	1	1	C. Non-Western state (non-Communist)
11	6	8	5	D. Other, DK, N.A.
24	14	19	13	E. None
14	8	0	0	F. West Germany, divided Germany
173	100%	147	100%	

| Germany | | France | | Code |
N	%	N	%	
				Q. 63. What kind of a threat is this?
62	46	89	59	A. Military threat
53	40	4	3	B. Communist competition
2	2	15	10	C. Economic depression
3	2	20	13	D. Domestic political upheaval
2	2	2	1	E. DK
1	1	16	11	F. None (on first response); other; slow growth of developing countries
11	8	0	0	G. Exposed position of Berlin; isolation through mistaken West German policy on Germany
0	0	6	4	H. U.S. economic penetration
134	101%	152	101%	
39		15		Not ascertained
173		127		No second threat given
346		294		

Germany		France		Code
N	%	N	%	
				Q. 65. In what form is there a military threat?
27	22	79	33	A. Possible involvement in world nuclear war
0	0	6	3	B. Possible involvement in limited war outside Europe
45	36	81	34	C. Possible involvement in a limited war in Europe
1	1	34	14	D. Weapons advance
47	38	36	15	E. No military threat (on first response)
5	4	2	1	F. DK, all forms
125	101%	238	100%	
48		15		Not ascertained
173		70		No second form given
173		118		No third form given
519		441		

Germany		France		Code
N	%	N	%	
				Q. 66. In your opinion, what would be the best defense against this threat?
1	1	12	5	A. National conventional arms
0	0	50	19	B. National nuclear arms
66	68	114	43	C. Alliance in conventional and/or nuclear arms
0	0	7	3	D. Integrated European conventional forces (supranational command)
0	0	33	12	E. Integrated European national forces
2	2	25	9	F. Complete integration of all European defense forces
3	3	6	2	G. Integration of nuclear forces of Atlantic community
8	8	13	5	H. Integration of all defense forces of Atlantic community
17	18	4	2	K. Miscellaneous
97	100%	264	100%	
76		7		Not ascertained
173		57		No second defense given
173		113		No third defense given
519		441		

Germany		France		
N	%	N	%	Code

Q. 67. It is often said that a national deterrent is a prerequisite of a country's independence. Do you share this view?

26	15	61	43	A. Yes
2	1	4	3	B. DK
143	84	76	54	C. No
171		141		
2		6		Not ascertained
173		147		

Q. 68. Is an independent deterrent a condition for German national independence? (Asked in France only.)

		3	2	A. Yes
		6	5	B. DK
		114	93	C. No
		123	100%	
		24		Not ascertained
		147		

Q. 69. Is a national deterrent a condition of French independence in particular? (Asked in Germany only.)

29	17			A. Yes
12	7			B. DK, N. A.
132	76			C. No
173	100%			

| Germany | | France | | Code |
N	%	N	%	
				Q. 70. Is an independent deterrent necessary for a nation's prestige in the world? (In Germany: In what sense would a national deterrent affect the Federal Republic's prestige in the world?
6	4	43	34	A. Yes, increase prestige
4	3	4	3	B. DK, evasive
156	94	79	63	C. No effect upon prestige; negative effect upon prestige
166	101%	126	100%	
7		21		Not ascertained
173		147		
				Q. 71. Is an independent deterrent worth the cost?
4	3	63	46	A. Yes
3	3	11	8	B. DK
156	95	64	46	C. No, evasive
163	101%	138	100%	
10		9		Not ascertained
173		147		
				Q. 72. Is (would) a national deterrent (be) credible to (Germany's) (France's) enemies?
31	31	46	34	A. Yes
64	63	75	56	B. No
6	6	14	11	C. DK
101	100%	135	101%	
72		12		Not ascertained
173		147		

Germany		France		
N	%	N	%	Code

Q. 73. What would happen to the force de frappe if de Gaulle left the political scene? (Asked in France only.)

		33	24	A. Force would be kept and strengthened
		70	52	B. Force would be supranational-ized
		9	7	C. Force would be abandoned
		23	17	D. DK
		135	100%	
		12		Not ascertained
		147		

Q. 74. If de Gaulle and his force de frappe should disappear what would be the effect on Germany? (Asked in Germany only.)

56	47			A. None
29	25			B. Generally beneficial effect
8	7			C. Generally detrimental effect, would enhance the necessity for German acquisition of nuclear arms
8	7			D. Would move Germany closer to the U.S.A.
17	14			E. DK
118	100%			
55				Not ascertained
173				

Germany		France		Code
N	%	N	%	

Q. 75. To what extent would (Germany's) (France's) military security ultimately depend upon the American deterrent? (In many of the German interviews, the phrase "even in the presence of a national deterrent" was added.)

121	76	23	17	A. Ultimately depends completely upon American deterrent
35	22	82	60	B. Ultimately depends in large measure upon American deterrent
2	1	28	20	C. Ultimately depends upon American deterrent only to a limited extent; DK
1	1	4	3	D. Does not depend at all upon American deterrent; American deterrent decreases (Germany's) (France's) security
159	100%	137	100%	
14		10		Not ascertained
173		147		

Germany		France		Code
N	%	N	%	
				Q. 76. In which circumstances do you think America will use her deterrent?
92	60	51	34	A. Will use against Communists and to protect any of its European allies
11	7	31	21	B. Will use to protect only certain of its European allies
9	6	55	36	C. Will use only to protect United States or North America
7	5	0	0	D. Will not use deterrent in any circumstances (on first response)
13	8	0	0	E. Will use as result of escalation
22	14	14	9	F. DK (on first response)
154	100%	151	100%	
19		34		Not ascertained
173		109		No second circumstance given
346		294		

Germany		France		Code
N	%	N	%	

Q. 78. Do you think it is likely that the United States will some day abandon its commitments for the defense of Western Europe?

Germany		France		Code
0	0	1	1	A. Likely
23	15	10	10	B. Likely under some conditions
1	1	12	12	C. Undecided; DK
10	6	13	13	D. Unlikely given certain conditions
124	79	66	65	E. Unlikely
158	101%	102	101%	
15		45		Not ascertained
173		147		

Q. 79. Do you think that efforts should be made to halt the proliferation of nuclear weapons to countries that do not now possess them?

Germany		France		Code
152	90	103	78	A. Yes
5	3	19	14	B. DK; undecided
13	8	10	8	C. No; impossible in reality
170	101%	132	100%	
3		15		Not ascertained
173		147		

Germany		France		Code
N	%	N	%	
				Q. 80. In your view, which countries should possess nuclear weapons?
14	9	19	14	A. No countries, few as possible, none if possible
3	2	0	0	B. U.S. only
50	32	18	13	C. U.S. and U.S.S.R. only, all countries that possess them at present except France
60	39	85	63	D. All countries that possess them at present
7	5	6	4	E. All countries that possess them at present plus Germany; all countries that want them and can afford them
13	8	2	1	F. Other, DK; this is all wishful thinking, unrealistic
6	4	0	0	G. U.S. and NATO, NATO and SEATO; U.S., U.S.S.R., Britain, and NATO
1	1	4	3	H. U.S. and unified Europe, unified Europe; U.S., U.S.S.R., unified Europe
154	100%	134	98%	
19		13		Not ascertained
173		147		

Germany		France		Code
N	%	N	%	
				Q. 82. Would you favor a European nuclear force independent of NATO?
10	6	53	40	A. Favor
23	14	43	32	B. Favor conditionally (if certain conditions prevail or develop)
0	0	15	11	C. Indifferent; undecided; DK
1	1	7	5	D. Oppose conditionally (if certain conditions prevail or develop)
134	80	16	12	E. Oppose
168	101%	134	101%	
5		13		Not ascertained
173		147		
				Q. 83. What do you think of a conventionally equipped European army? Would you favor the EDC today?
54	35	12	23	A. Favor
17	11	16	31	B. Favor conditionally (if certain conditions prevail or develop; including "too late now")
7	5	8	16	C. Indifferent; undecided; DK
7	5	6	12	D. Oppose conditionally (if certain conditions prevail or develop)
67	45	9	18	E. Oppose
152	101%	51	100%	
21		96		Not ascertained
173		147		

Germany		France		Code
N	%	N	%	

Q. 84. The U.S.A. and Russia recently concluded a bilateral agreement banning nuclear testing in the atmosphere. Do you approve or disapprove of this East/West agreement?

143	86	63	46	A. Approve
15	9	12	9	B. Approve conditionally (if certain conditions prevail or develop)
4	2	36	27	C. Indifferent; undecided; DK
0	0	7	5	D. Disapprove conditionally (if certain conditions prevail or develop)
5	3	18	13	E. Disapprove
167	100%	136	100%	
6		11		Not ascertained
173		147		

Q. 85. How do you feel about (Germany) (France) not being consulted?

79	50	44	36	A. Country should have been consulted
77	48	73	59	B. Makes no difference whether country was consulted or not; country should not have been consulted
3	2	6	5	C. DK
159	100%	123	100%	
14		24		Not ascertained
173		147		

Germany		France		Code
N	%	N	%	

Q. 86. Would you favor further arms control agreements between the U.S. and the U.S.S.R.?

Germany		France		Code
139	84	70	52	A. Favor
20	12	27	20	B. Favor conditionally (if certain conditions prevail or develop)
2	1	30	22	C. Indifferent; undecided; DK
1	1	2	2	D. Oppose conditionally (if certain conditions prevail or develop)
3	2	5	4	E. Oppose
165	100%	134	100%	
8		13		Not ascertained
173		147		

Q. 88. Would you favor further arms control agreements even if your country is not consulted?

Germany		France		Code
99	65	71	55	A. Yes
21	14	13	10	B. Yes, conditionally (if certain conditions prevail or develop)
1	1	39	30	C. Indifferent; undecided; DK
0	0	2	2	D. No, conditionally
31	20	4	3	E. No
152	100%	129	100%	
21		18		Not ascertained
173		147		

| Germany | | France | | Code |
N	%	N	%	
				Q. 89. For years both East and West have been offering alternative schemes for arms control and disarmament, some of them dealing with problems of arms control in Europe and others more universal in scope. Of which of these have you heard most?
20	7	21	11	A. General and complete disarmament
24	8	9	5	B. Complete destruction; freeze in production; reduction of nuclear weapons stockpiles
19	7	5	3	C. Complete elimination of conventional weapons; freeze in production of conventional weapons: neutralization of other areas in the world; other plans
105	37	34	18	D. De-nuclearization of Central Europe; troop withdrawal in Central Europe; neutralization of Central Europe
48	17	19	10	E. Ban on atomic testing; inspection of weapons
44	15	8	4	F. DK (on first response)
18	6	75	41	G. Heard of all or most (on first response)
7	3	14	8	H. Heard of no arms control plans in particular (on first response)
285	100%	185	100%	
10		17		Not ascertained
99		119		No second plan given
125		120		No third plan given
519		441		

Germany		France		Code
N	%	N	%	
				Q. 90. Which of the various arms control and disarmament plans would you favor?
17	9	13	8	A. General and complete disarmament
20	11	35	20	B. Complete destruction; freeze in production of nuclear weapons; reduction of nuclear weapons stockpiles
8	4	5	3	C. Complete elimination; freeze in production; reduction of conventional weapons; neutralization of other areas in the world; U.S. plans for disarmament in stages
30	16	10	6	D. De-nuclearization of, troop withdrawal from, neutralization of Central Europe
35	18	33	19	E. Ban on atomic testing; inspection of weapons
44	23	8	5	F. DK (on first response)
5	3	17	10	G. Any and all plans (on first response)
32	17	52	30	H. Favors no plans (on first response)
191	101%	173	101%	
13		23		Not ascertained
151		118		No second plan given
164		127		No third plan given
519		441		

| Germany | | France | | Code |
N	%	N	%	

Q. 91. Would the de-nuclearization of Central Europe ease the threat of military conflict there?

Germany		France		
47	29	16	25	A. Yes
10	6	8	12	B. DK
104	65	41	63	C. No; on the contrary, would increase danger
161	100%	65	100%	
12		82		Not ascertained
173		147		

Q. 92. What do you think about the complete neutralization of Central Europe?

Germany		France		
10	6	7	10	A. Favor
23	14	13	18	B. Favor conditionally (if certain conditions prevail or develop)
4	2	13	18	C. Indifferent; undecided, DK
2	1	11	15	D. Oppose conditionally (if certain conditions prevail or develop)
127	77	27	38	E. Oppose, utopian
166	100%	71	99%	
7		76		Not ascertained
173		147		

| Germany | | France | | Code |
N	%	N	%	
				Q. 93. Should foreign troops be withdrawn from both Eastern and Western Europe?
12	7	2	2	A. Favor withdrawal
25	15	14	16	B. Favor conditionally (if certain conditions prevail or develop)
4	2	7	8	C. Indifferent, undecided, DK
5	3	11	13	D. Oppose conditionally (if certain conditions prevail or develop)
119	72	53	61	E. Oppose
165	99%	87	100%	
8		60		Not ascertained
173		147		
				Q. 94. Should an East-West agreement on arms control be coupled with inspection?
127	78	38	38	A. Yes
17	10	13	13	B. Yes, conditionally (if certain conditions prevail or develop)
11	7	47	47	C. Indifferent, undecided, DK
4	2	0	0	D. No conditionally (if certain conditions prevail or develop)
4	2	1	1	E. No
163	99%	99	99%	
10		48		Not ascertained
173		147		

Germany		France		Code
N	%	N	%	
				Q. 98. Do you think it is possible to ease international tension by disarmament, or is the whole question of disarmament and arms control a mere utopia not worth discussing?
131	77	61	49	A. Disarmament is definitely worth discussing (progress can be made)
0	0	25	20	B. Disarmament is utopian, but worth discussing anyway
17	10	17	14	C. Disarmament is worth discussing, but not at the present time
0	0	0	0	D. DK
22	13	22	18	E. Disarmament is a utopian scheme not worth discussing
170	100%	125	101%	
3		22		Not ascertained
173		147		

Index

ABC weapons, 80

ACD, see Arms control and disarmament

Age, as determinant of political attitude in France and Germany, 14

Age groups, attitudes and expectations of:
France and Germany, 44-51, 68-71, 78; junior elites, 46
France, 23-24, 47, 48, 62, 68, 69-70; and prospects for French politics, 71-74; junior elites, 23, 58-59, 62, 63, 66, 69-70, 70 n, 72, 75; mid-elites, 23, 58-59, 62-63, 69-70, 72, 75; senior elites, 23, 58-59, 62, 66, 69-71, 75
Germany, 45, 47-48, 49, 61, 62; and prospects for West German politics, 74-75; junior elites, 45, 47, 49, 53, 59, 61, 65, 66, 70 n; mid-elites, 53, 59, 61, 62, 63, 65; senior elites, 59, 61, 62, 63, 65
variance in, due to age, 68, 69-70, 75

Agricultural issue, in France and Germany, 102

Aid, cost of, as source of French and German friction with U.S., 114

Alienated, alienation; among French elites, 24; among French and German elites, especially toward foreign policy, 55-57

Alker, Hayward R., Jr., viii

Alliance, alliances: French and German elite support for, as basis of Western European security, 1, 2-9 (table), 11-12, 95, 108, 109, 128; French elite support for cooperation in, 11, 22, 23, 70; and influence of proalliance elites in France, 71-72; German elite support for, 24; problems of, 77; in questionnaire, 85

Alliance, East Germany, with Soviet bloc, 34

Alliance with United States: French and German elite and mass acceptance of, 15; French dependence on, 74; dilemmas over, 79; German support for, after deGaulle, 24

Alliance, Western, vi, 78, 80, 81; extension of, 78; British, French, German, mass support for in peacetime vs. war, 20; French and German mass images of, 20, 21; French electoral support for deGaulle's attack on, vi; lack of cross-national communication within, 43; see also North Atlantic Treaty Organization (NATO)

Allied consensus, 76; decision-making and risk-sharing, 77

Ally, allies: French-German reliance on each other now, 97, 125; after deGaulle, 97, 98

145